English Men of Letters

EDITED BY J. C. SQUIRE

THOMAS LOVE PEACOCK

THE MACMILLAN COMPANY
NEW YORK · BOSTON · CHICAGO · DALLAS
ATLANTA · SAN FRANCISCO

MACMILLAN & CO., LIMITED
LONDON · BOMBAY · CALCUTTA
MELBOURNE

THE MACMILLAN CO. OF CANADA, LTD.
TORONTO

THOMAS LOVE PEACOCK

BY

J. B. PRIESTLEY

New York

THE MACMILLAN COMPANY

1927

PRINTED IN THE UNITED STATES OF AMERICA
BY THE FERRIS PRINTING COMPANY

PREFACE

In the biographical chapters of this study I have taken toll of the usual authorities, but I should like to acknowledge my special indebtedness to Mr. Carl van Doren's extremely valuable *Life of Thomas Love Peacock*. I am sorry that this biography is now out of print. I must also regret that the concluding volumes of Messrs. Constable's fine Halliford Edition of the complete works, volumes that may possibly contain a little new material, were not to hand while I was writing these chapters. I can hardly imagine, however, that such material would interfere with any judgment on Peacock's character or work to be found there. In the account of Seithenyn in Chapter VII., I have been compelled to repeat several sentences from my essay on this figure in *The English Comic Characters*, and I can only hope that this will be regarded as a mark of consistency and not of indolence.

J. B. P.

19936

CONTENTS

CHAPTER VII

CHAPTER VIII

THOMAS LOVE PEACOCK

CHAPTER I

Among the London merchants in the directory for 1778 is one Samuel Peacock of the Glass Warehouse, Holborn Bridge. There was also another Peacock, Thomas, in the glass trade, and the two firms were united in 1784 as Samuel and Thomas Peacock, 46 Holborn Bridge. Four years later the senior partner died, and the firm became George and Thomas Peacock and afterwards Peacock and Roper. This Samuel Peacock, glass merchant, was the father of the novelist. Beyond the fact that he was engaged in this business during these years, and that he left his widow fairly well provided for, we know nothing about him. Peacock is not a common name, but it is found in various parts of England and Scotland. From a note made by his widow later, we know that Samuel had his son baptized by Dr. Hunter of the Scotch Kirk, London Wall, but that is not sufficient evidence that he himself was a Scot. The father may have been as whimsical and unconventional as the son and, though English, may have preferred the Scotch Kirk just as his son preferred to stay outside any church. If there was any Scots blood in the novelist, he certainly contrived to subdue it during a literary career in which he continually made Scotsmen and their favourite diversions, from

1

historical romance to political economy, the targets of his wit.

Fortunately we know a great deal more about Peacock's mother than we do about his father, and it was his mother who was the dominating influence in his early life. Sarah Love belonged to a Devon family and was the eldest daughter, born in 1754, of Thomas Love, a master in the Royal Navy who served under Lord Rodney and finally lost a leg in the West Indian naval victory over the French in 1782. He had already retired from the sea and was settled at Chertsey when his daughter gave birth to a son, an event that she records for us in an attestation drawn up some forty years afterwards:

I hereby certify that my son Thomas Love Peacock was born on the eighteenth day of October in the year of Our Lord One Thousand Seven Hundred and Eighty Five, at a quarter past two in the morning, at Weymouth in Dorsetshire.

She returned from Weymouth, which she had probably visited for reasons of health, to London, where the child was baptized three months later, and she remained there until after her husband's death in 1788. The following twelve years she and her son passed with Thomas Love at Chertsey. Thus, Samuel Peacock and the glass business and London vanish from the story the moment after they are introduced into it, for at the age of three Thomas Love Peacock is taken out of London and spends his most impressionable years in the country, under the care of a widowed mother and an old sea-dog of a grandfather. They lived together in a cottage named Gogmoor Hall.

There is about this Gogmoor Hall (even in the very name, with its air of improbability) a faint suggestion of those other fantastic Halls and Castles that Peacock was afterwards to call into existence for his and our good pleasure. To begin with, it was set in those exquisitely rural surroundings, miles from the smoke and bustle of a town, that Peacock always delighted in and used, as a backcloth at least, for his comedies. Chertsey, twenty-two miles up the river from London, is still a very charming place, and in those days, when for all its weekly market and four annual fairs it had less than three thousand inhabitants, it was probably really beautiful, a day-dream of rural peace, with a noble sweep of river, wooded hills, deep pastures, trim lawns and a few streets of honestly built houses, for ever catching the eye. Beautiful or not, it certainly gave Peacock one of his few genuine enthusiasms, namely, a lifelong passion for country air and country scenes, and with it a corresponding distaste for cities. He gives us an idyllic sketch of some sides of life at Chertsey in the paper he wrote, half a century later, for *Bentley's Miscellany* called *Recollections of Childhood: The Abbey House*. This house, built on the site of the old Abbey during the Restoration, was the local mansion and the home of the Barwell family, who were connected with the East India Company. The young son, Charles, was a schoolfellow and playmate of Peacock's, so that there were many exchanges of visits. Peacock's picture of life at the Abbey House is probably idealised—it was one of his favourite tricks, this idealising of the past for the purpose of satirising the present—but there is enough truth in its description of a leisured ease and tranquillity, of open-handed

country gentlemen and quiet country ladies, to suggest
the atmosphere of life at Chertsey in the later eighteenth
century. As he grew up, he spent a great deal of his
time walking the neighbouring countryside, and had a
special fondness for the more solitary places. "I was
early given to long walks and rural explorations," he
tells us, "and there was scarcely a spot of the Park or
the Forest (Windsor) with which I was not intimately
acquainted. There were two very different scenes to
which I was especially attached—Virginia Water, and
a dell near Winkfield Plain." He was always attached
to such places, but he was not always able to indulge
in the pleasure of revisiting many of them, for as time
passed either they were enclosed, as the Park came to
be later, or, like Virginia Water, they became too
popular, to the manifest indignation of the novelist, who
very characteristically resented being kept out himself
and equally resented other people being there with him.
While he was a boy, however, he had all the rural
solitude he wanted.

The inmates of Gogmoor Hall may not have been so
typically Peacockian as its setting, but nevertheless they
formed an unusual little company. We know very
little about the head of the household, old Thomas Love,
but it is not difficult to imagine what the retired
sailor was like, particularly as we do know that Captain
Hawltaught in *Melincourt* was sketched from him.
That patron and friend of Sir Oran was a retired sailor
too, and had an Illyrian fondness for cakes and ale
and catches and a contempt for water-drinkers and all
the Malvolios of this world. Thomas Love was clearly
of this type, a fine old crusted sea-dog, filled with
humorous crotchets and liquor, and with a sailor's hearty

dislike of all mere theory-spinning, truth-hunting,
Utopia-building. It is not surprising that his grand-
son soon came to share many of his tastes.

For Peacock, however, the most important person
in that house was the mother who, losing her husband so
soon and having only one child, naturally played a great
part in that child's life. Peacock and his mother were
the happiest and most intimate of companions to the
very end of her life. When she died, in 1833, he
declared that the loss of her, to whom he had read all
his books before they were published, had taken the
heart out of his writing. All this may seem rather
strange, particularly when we consider the nature of
those books, but then Mrs. Peacock was an unusual
woman, very far removed from the sentimental, tearful,
widowed mother, the female of sensibility, whose figure
may be found in the popular fiction of her time. She
could turn a verse or two, and was above all a reader,
having a taste for solid books, especially history.
Gibbon was always by her side, a fact that tells us
more about her than pages of anecdote. A boy who,
left fatherless, has for years the close companionship
of a mother who enjoys solid reading and delights in
Gibbon, is likely to grow up with certain strongly
marked tastes if he should be himself fond of books.
It is not given to every one to make acquaintance with
Epicureanism and irony at his mother's knee.

Growing up in this household of adults and spending most of his time either reading or going for solitary
rambles, Thomas Love Peacock showed himself a
clever precocious little boy. He spent six and a half
years at the only school he ever attended, at Englefield
Green, and was highly praised for his work there, though

he was only twelve when he left, bearing with him at
least a nodding acquaintance with Greek, Latin and
French. There is a letter of his, written when he was
eleven and probably addressed to the master at school
and not to a genuine correspondent, that is evidence
enough of his droll precocity. It begins:

DEAR SIR—The present alarming state of the country
points out the subject of a letter from me to you. At this
time, threatened by a powerful and victorious enemy, and
bending under a load of severe exactions, I take up my pen
to give you my sentiments. Though I do not wish Mr.
Pitt's removal from his exalted station, yet I think he would
have acted more in conformity with the sentiments of the
People had he taxed every one according to their income.
I think, too, he was wrong to begin this war, but much
more to refuse peace when the French demanded it, since
which time we have suffered so many losses and now vainly
endeavour to extricate ourselves from a war in which his
imprudence involves us. . . .

It is not difficult to catch a glimpse, behind these pompous
phrases, of an anxious pen-biting small boy, but it is also
not difficult to see that he was no ordinary small boy.

Had it not been for his precocity, we should never
have known what happened to him during the years
immediately after he left school, but he chanced to win
a prize and find his way into print. Early in 1800, a
curious publication known as *The Monthly Preceptor* in
its periodical form and as *The Juvenile Library* when
it was bound into volumes, came out to give young
students "A Complete Course of Instruction on every
useful subject: particularly Natural and Experimental
Philosophy, Moral Philosophy, Natural History, Botany,
Ancient and Modern History, Biography and the Manners and Customs of Nations, Ancient and Modern

Languages, English Law, Penmanship, Mathematics, and the Belles Lettres". The Prize Productions of competing young students were to be printed, and there was to be monthly distribution of prizes to the value of fifteen guineas and upwards. One of the young students to win prizes in the very first number, for a poetical answer to the question, "Is History or Biography the more improving Study?", is "Master T. L. Peacock, aged 14", who is declared by Messrs. Ludlow, Fraser & Co., merchants of Angel Court, Throgmorton Street, to be employed by them as a clerk, to be only fourteen, and to have been entirely unassisted in his composition. Among his fellow-prizewinners in this competition is another precocious youth, Leigh Hunt. The twenty-odd stilted heroic couplets, in which Master Peacock preferred History to Biography, were not, the *Monthly Preceptor* admitted, of any great poetical value, but it was held that they constituted "an extraordinary effort of genius in a boy of this age; and as such the Proprietors have rewarded him with an *extra prize,* viz. an elementary book, value 5s". The other prize was "Elegant Extracts in Verse epitomised".

We know then that Peacock was in London in the early part of 1800, in the service of a firm of merchants, but we do not know when he went there, exactly what he did, nor when he finally left. Probably he disliked his office work, wished to do nothing but read hard and write verse, and so protested to his mother, who was not without means and sympathised with his desires. It may be that the prize turned the scale. All that we do know is that he remained in London for the next few years, and, having left the City, devoted himself to the pleasant task of completing his education in his own way. He turned a shelf of books, whether at home or in the reading-room of the British Museum, into his school and university. "I took to reading the best books, illustrated by the best critics," he has told us. Those were the days when vast schemes of reading—Latin and Greek in the morning, French in the afternoon, Italian in the evening, and so forth—were very often planned by young men of leisure. The early years of the last century would seem to have been filled with diligent young gentlemen who divided their time between serious and methodical reading and feats of pedestrianism. Peacock was of this company even in his teens. He became an enthusiastic student of the humanities, with all the tastes and pursuits of a hard-reading university man of the period, so that by the time he was of an age to begin academic life, he was a ripe candidate for honours at Oxford or Cambridge. We do not know whether he wanted to go to a university or not. All that we do know is that he did not go, and that, like so many men who stayed outside to do their own reading in their own way, he never missed an opportunity afterwards of congratulating himself on his escape. It is possible that he wanted to go, but that, being in no position to win a scholarship, he was persuaded by his family that their means would not allow of such a step and was offered a few years' freedom, a much less expensive matter, as a consolation. It is equally possible, however, that he had not the slightest desire to enter a university and merely pleased himself, for there was always a decided strain of independence, sometimes amounting to sheer wilfulness, in his character, and though his tastes were scholarly, he had little inclination towards official scholarship. He liked to read seriously and hard, but he also preferred to choose his own authors, thus occupying a middle position between the desultory if enthusiastic reader and the close methodical scholar.

The fact that he never went to a university and was left to educate himself is very important. It does not explain everything about him, as some of his critics would have us believe, but it does explain a great deal. It explains those gibes at Oxford and Cambridge that are scattered so freely throughout the novels, in which the academic life, as opposed to the free pursuits and unprejudiced interests of the solitary scholar, is attacked as a mere waste of time and energy. Apart from these frequent sarcasms, which, after all, occur in places where everything under the sun is similarly pilloried, he did seriously maintain that universities, at least in England, were futile where they were not definitely harmful in their influence, particularly where men of uncommon ability were concerned. His criticism is by no means absurd and very few of his sarcasms are entirely wide of the mark, but it is always obvious that his attitude towards the question rests on a prejudice and that nowhere is he stating the whole case but is simply acting as Devil's Advocate. His attacks would have been more successful if they had come from within those universities and not from outside. Moreover, though it is true enough that Oxford and Cambridge have loosed upon the world a large number of scholars who were inferior to the solitary Peacock, it is also true that they have produced a considerable number of better scholars than Peacock, and if they are to take the blame for the first, they must be allowed to have the credit for the second.

If this were all, however, the fact would not be important. But it explains a great deal more than his attitude towards the two universities of which he could never claim membership. Thus it explains, in part, that surprising vein of pedantry to be found in Peacock, particularly in his criticism of other men's work. He was easy-going enough with his own translations and Greek accents, and never hesitated to take liberties with his material (as, for example, with the Welsh legends that he used for *The Misfortunes of Elphin*), yet he could seriously condemn the work of his fellow-authors because it contained some little slip or trifled with antique authority, denouncing Keats, for example, because he "could prove by a hundred quotations that the sleep of Endymion was eternal, whereas in the modern poem the Latmian shepherd is for ever capering up and down the earth and ocean like the German chaser of shadows". This carping pedantic strain, as we shall presently see, is nearly always present in his criticism and considerably reduces its value. Why should it have been there at all? In most matters Peacock was anything but a narrow pedant, was indeed the enemy of all such. His was certainly not the formal mind. No doubt his attitude is partly explained by his prejudice, which grew with the years and was a curiously mixed product that will be examined later in this survey, against the poetry of his own time, especially the more romantic poetry. But it is also explained by the fact that, not having acquired his learning in the usual way, he was always tempted to brandish it in the faces of those who had. He might be said to have been the graduate of a new and un-recognised university, his own, and so to have worn his gown self-consciously and rather aggressively. Thus he liked to air his knowledge and, if possible, to trap the complacent collegians. Moreover, having found his own way into the enchanted gardens of the ancient world, he could not help having a rather proprietorial and jealous feeling about them, and so tended to resent any intrusion, especially that of persons who had not found their way in, but, perched like some Keats or other on top of a Lemprière, were peeping over the wall. There are times when he obviously regards classical culture as a kind of secret society, and in spite of his numerous gibes at little dons, he cannot be entirely freed from the charge of being donnish himself.

If he had gone up to Oxford or Cambridge, he might easily have become a don and have given up to the common-room what was meant for mankind. So far we have dwelt on the disadvantages of his self-educa-tion, but these are far outweighed by the advantages. He read what he wanted to read, and was able to dis-regard everything that did not interest him. No examination loomed before him to turn his authors at last into so many tasks. The ancient comedies he delighted in never became for him a mere "subject." The natural result of this is a certain gusto in his scholarship, the gusto of the amateur, which found its way into his own more characteristic work. A more formal education might have encouraged him to put life and literature into two separate compartments, to make a distinction between his interests in the library and his interests in the world outside. He might have merely become a critical authority on his favourite authors, but as it was he absorbed their spirit and tended to see life as they did. He had a passion, as we know, for Aristophanes, but other men have had this passion, men who knew more about the comic poet than ever Peacock did. But these others, critics and scholars, have simply kept their Aristophanes in the library, whereas Peacock, we may say, brought him out into the world by giving us what can only be described as Aristophanic fiction. He always tended to become a disciple not a student, an enthusiast not an authority. Pleasing himself in his reading, he was able to feed his temperament. What is unusual in him is his combination of bookishness and a knowledge of life; he may be regarded as a scholar thrust out into the world, or a man of the world let loose among books, and as either he is an original. It is not difficult to see why the fact that he was allowed to go his own way and did not "finish his education" (a phrase he frequently mocked at) is very significant.

But the Peacock we have been discussing is the mature man and not the youth who spent the opening years of the last century reading hard in London and occasionally scribbling verses. Of these verses the most important are *The Monks of St. Mark,* which was written in 1804, and was probably printed, though no record remains of it in pamphlet form, and *Palmyra,* the title piece of a small volume that appeared in 1806. The first, a slap-dash affair, describes the monks at their liquor and is full of rough-and-tumble incident, ending very characteristically with the lines:

They reel'd back to their bowls, laughed at care and foul weather,
And were shortly all under the table together.

But it is only interesting because it gives us a hint, the only one we are given for some time, of Peacock's characteristic manner. The other poem, *Palmyra,* is in the manner that Peacock was to cultivate for some years, before he discovered his true vein. It is a piece of tepid high-falutin' of the kind that Peacock himself came to despise most heartily in later life. Having read Wood's *Ruins of Palmyra,* an account of a visit to the ruined city of the desert, the young poet proceeds to meditate upon fallen greatness in the conventional manner of the time:

> Yet faithful MEMORY's raptur'd eye
> Can still the godlike form descry,

and so forth. As was usual in such poems, there were far more footnotes than verse, and the honest prose of the travellers and historians who are quoted is better reading than the poet's frigid talk of "Meek SCIENCE too, and Taste refin'd". Six years later the poem was revised and considerably improved, and this later version had among its admirers no less a person than Shelley.

The head of the Chertsey household, Thomas Love, died at the end of 1805, and shortly afterwards Peacock returned there. We know from a letter written two years later that he spent the autumn of 1806 on a visit, probably a walking tour, to Scotland. This letter was written to Edward Hookham, the son of Thomas Hookham, bookseller and publisher, whose "Literary Assembly" was a meeting-place for minor literati. The two young men became good friends, went off on tours together, and frequently corresponded, Peacock asking for various books to be sent to him and discussing the publication of a new volume of verse he was planning. In the summer of 1807 he fell in love with a girl of eighteen who lived near by, Fanny Falkner, and the two of them used to meet at the ruins of Newark Abbey. It was not long before twenty-two was engaged to eighteen, nor much longer before the engagement, which did not meet with the approval of certain relatives, was broken off. Fanny was married in haste to some one else, but died the very next year. This tragic episode in his life, so curiously reminiscent in its action and setting of the sentimental balladry of the time, left its mark on Peacock. It would be the idlest sentimentalism to pretend that ever afterwards he was a man with a secret sorrow, the familiar tragic clown of romantic fable, yet we have only to consider his attitude towards this brief passage in his life, with its swift, happy courtship and its double loss, to realise the extent, if not the exact nature, of its influence upon him. He married later and was happy in his marriage, and lived for sixty years after those meetings in Newark Abbey, yet he never forgot them, and, as we learn from his granddaughter, dreamed constantly of this long-lost sweetheart during the last few weeks of his life. All his days this avowed enemy of posturing sentiment wore a locket in which there was some of her hair. Setting aside the drinking songs, we find that his best verses have this episode for their subject. There is that little poem of three stanzas, "I dug, beneath the cypress shade", which was discovered after his death, but was evidently written about the time of these events, with its fine last verse:

> Frail as thy love, the flowers were dead
>   Ere yet the evening sun was set:
> But years shall see the cypress spread,
>   Immutable as my regret,

which is worth more than all his more ambitious performances of this period put together. Then, years afterwards, there was that poem called *Newark Abbey*, which appeared in *Fraser's* and was praised by Tennyson:

> I gaze where August's sunbeam falls
> Along these grey and lonely walls,
> Till in its light absorbed appears
> The lapse of five-and-thirty years,

a poem that tells over again this old-remembered joy and grief. Peacock had not a romantic imagination— and it was the mistake of his youth to imagine that he had—but he had a strong natural vein of sentiment, a current of feeling that was, as it were, driven underground by this catastrophe of his youth. It did not make its appearance again until late in life. It is significant, however, that in his fiction, in which so many things are mocked, there is no mockery of young love and simple affection, but only of ultra-romantic egoistical attitudes, on the one hand, and unnatural match-mongering, on the other.

Both his mother's brothers were in the Navy, and, late in 1808, they obtained for him a post as secretary to Sir Home Riggs Popham, of H.M.S. *Venerable*. He was able to take his leave of Chertsey for a time, but he soon found that a winter at sea was not to his taste. "As to writing poetry, or doing anything else that is rational in this floating inferno," he writes to Hookham, "it is almost next to a moral impossibility. I would give the world now to be at home, and devote the whole winter to the composition of a comedy." However, he contrived to write a little and to read a good deal, and actually made some progress with a long poem that he had had in mind for some time, *The Genius of the Thames.* The following March found him free again, and he spent the remainder of the year working away at his poem, which gave him an excellent excuse for some very pleasant rambling in Berkshire and Oxfordshire, following the river to its source. *The Genius of the Thames* was finished early in 1810, and published in the summer of that year, when *The Anti-Jacobin,* finding in it no disturbing touch of genius, praised it heartily at the expense of infinitely better work. Two years later a second edition was published. There is probably nothing duller in all literature than a long topographical poem, which, by dint of frigid and unscrupulous personification, turns geography, history and political economy into lumbering mock-poetry, and *The Genius of the Thames* is no exception, being a very long and excessively dull chain of poetical common-places. So far, we may say, Peacock is wasting his time.

When he had finished exploring the upper Thames valley, he decided to go farther afield, and shortly afterwards made a trip that was to have important consequences both for his life and his work. He paid his first visit to Wales, the home of his future wife and the land whose wild scenes and legends he put to such good uses in his fiction. It was winter when he first arrived there, staying at Maentwrog in Merionethshire, but he was so enchanted by the magnificent scenery of the district, which he explored very thoroughly, that he remained there some months. He became friendly with the local parson, Dr. Gryffydh, and even more friendly with the parson's daughter. Jane Gryffydh was an amiable and beautiful young creature, who could talk of "Scipio and Hannibal, and the Emperor Otho". His early relations

with her are very mysterious, and suggest that either
he was attracted but afraid of falling in love again, or
that, being in love, he was afraid of offering marriage.
What is certain is that they saw a good deal of one
another during his first visit to Wales, which was probably prolonged partly on her account, that he saw her
once more during the spring of the following year, and
that he did not set eyes on her again for another eight
years, although he actually did pay another visit to Wales
during that time.

Meanwhile, probably lovelorn but hesitant, he was
very much the poetical character, soliloquising on
remote mountain summits on the subject of wild nature
and poetic melancholy, during this period of his life,
which may be said to end with the publication, in
April 1812, of *The Philosophy of Melancholy*. This
poem, whose philosophy is almost non-existent and
whose melancholy is mostly literary affectation, is really
a justification of a life of solitude and "sensibility"
passed on or near the Welsh mountains. The spirit of
philosophic melancholy, we are given to understand,
enables the mind to escape the clutch of bitter circumstance, to see that discord is merely an illusion, to
comprehend that "all-perfect wisdom which arranges
the whole in harmony". The modern world, with
the aid of its sciences, its additional knowledge of truth,
has an advantage over the ancient world and should
attain to a greater height of stark virtue. It is difficult
to see the real Peacock in all this conventional moralising. In spite of its stilted heroic couplets and stock
imagery, however, the poem has some descriptive
passages, chiefly of the Welsh mountain scenery, that
are not bad examples of the formal picturesque in verse

and are an advance upon anything in *The Genius of the Thames*. Miss Gryffydh makes her appearance in the poem as

> . . . that fair form, ah! now too far remote!
> Whose glossy locks on ocean-breezes float;
> That tender voice, whose rapture-breathing thrill,
> Unheard so long, in fancy vibrates still;
> That Parian hand, that draws, with artless fire,
> The soul of music from her mountain-lyre,

and no doubt found some consolation in these grandiose references to her charms during the eight years in which she never once set eyes on her poetical admirer.

All this time the satirist in Peacock had been struggling with the romantic-sentimental versifier, and though apparently fighting a losing battle, finding his way more and more easily into the letters but hardly at all into published work, he had actually reached the eve of conquest. Though there was still another and longer poem to come, this year, 1812, marks Peacock's retreat from the Moscow of romance. It also marks, significantly, the beginnings of his association with a poet who was all romance. Peacock now steps out of his obscurity into the mingled moonlight and limelight that follow the life of Shelley. "I saw Shelley for the first time in 1812, just before he went to Tanyrallt," Peacock tells us. "I saw him again once or twice before I went to North Wales in 1813. On my return he was residing at Bracknell, and invited me to visit him there." They did not meet at Nant Gwillt, near Rhayador in Radnorshire, as some writers have asserted, because Peacock was not there during 1812 and did not visit the place until the following year. They were probably made known to one another by Hookham, some time in the autumn, when Shelley was in

London between his two visits to North Wales. During the winter they apparently exchanged letters (Peacock attacking the Welsh in verse), and it is significant that among the books that Shelley ordered are some of Peacock's favourites, Monboddo, Drummond and Horne Tooke. Meanwhile Peacock wrote a *Grammatico-Allegorical Ballad, Sir Hornbook; or, Childe Launcelot's Expedition,* a mock-ballad for children that contrives to give them instruction in the elements of grammar. Before spring Shelley had had his mysterious adventure with the unknown caller and had left Wales for Ireland. Peacock paid his other visit to North Wales and heard all about the famous adventure, and then spent some time during the summer in Leicestershire, where his unusual habits, reading two books at once (a Greek dramatist and a commentator), sailing paper boats, and taking long solitary walks, excited the wonder of the country people. By the end of the summer he was staying with the Shelleys at Bracknell; "a very mild, agreeable man, and a good scholar", his host writes of him; and when, at the conclusion of the visit, the Shelleys decided on a leisurely tour to Edinburgh, Peacock, in spite of his lack of enthusiasm and of the hostility of the Bracknell set, was invited to go with them. The famous friendship, which brought together the two extremes of English Literature, had now begun.

The respective works of Shelley and Peacock reveal two minds so strongly opposed to one another that their friendship has been a puzzle to many people. But such people are seeing the two men against the background of eternity rather than the background of their own time and place. We are apt to forget that

even the most eccentric or towering genius is compelled
to lead some sort of social life, making friends, rather
casually like the rest of us, as he goes along. If we
think of Peacock and Shelley as they were when they
first met, if we see them against the ordinary hurly-
burly of social life, we shall realise that there were many
reasons why they should have become so friendly. The
difference in their ages, nearly seven years, was not
great enough to form a barrier between them. They
were both young men who were unfettered and
unconventional, devoted to literature, and with a
common passion for Greek. "His enthusiasm is not
very ardent," Shelley writes of Peacock, "nor his
views very comprehensive; but he is neither superstitious, ill-tempered, dogmatical, or proud." To the
Shelley of twenty, Peacock seemed a considerable poet:
the conclusion of the revised version of *Palmyra* he
called "the finest piece of poetry I ever read". The
scholarship of the older man appealed to the ardent
student in Shelley. Peacock, on his side, was not so
wedded to solitude that he could not welcome a
companion with whom to walk and talk, particularly
as his one friend, Hookham, was tied to London most
of the year. His friendship may have been less disinterested, for Shelley's hospitality and occasional gifts
of money probably helped to consolidate it, but it is
easily explained by the likeness in habits and interests,
the common passion for long rambles and Greek
dramatists, and the accessibility (an important condition of friendship that is frequently overlooked) of
this new companion. It is absurdly unjust to see in
Peacock the sneering sponger discovered by some of
Shelley's more fervent admirers, who have an odd

trick of reviling all his friends. Peacock came to regard his young companion with a cool, humorous and sceptical eye, seeing him (as most of us would have done had he actually lived with us and not merely flashed, splendidly and tragically, through our imagination) as a comic figure, a shrill and fantastic young man with a weakness for intellectual flirtation, not a beautiful young poet doomed to die in his high noon. He mistrusted and ridiculed the type Shelley, but that does not mean that he had not a genuine goodwill towards the individual Shelley, for whom he performed, in spite of serious differences, many useful offices to the very last. Shelley himself, as his letters show, regarded Peacock as one of the few, the very few, friends left him in England, and we have no right to quarrel with his judgment.

This association has been discussed over and over again in connection with Shelley, and it cannot be lightly dismissed now that Peacock holds the centre of the stage. The direct influence of either man upon the other can easily be over-estimated, but the consequences of this friendship, the result of indirect influence, were of immense importance for Peacock. As yet uncertain of his aim, toying half-heartedly with the sentimental-romantic, he came to learn what he could do and what he could not do. This friendship discovered for him the true bent of his mind. Shelley provided a touch-stone for genuine romantic feeling, and it did not take long for Peacock to realise that so far he himself had only been playing the romantic enthusiast. His best verse was still to come, yet it is perhaps true to say that his friend's blaze of poetical genius nearly withered the poet in him and ripened the satirist. Up to this time he had spent most of his adult life in solitude and so it had not been difficult for him to entertain a wrong idea of himself and his powers, to see himself as a creature of philosophic melancholy, to indulge in a little high-falutin' when the opportunity offered itself. But now, in the society of Shelley and his friends, where enthusiasm raged day and night, where the wildest romanticism, far surpassing his, was in full flower, he began to entertain certain doubts and scruples, and, as tempting targets multiplied day by day, began to sharpen the arrows of his wit. All this naturally took time, yet if there can be said to be a certain moment when Peacock the satirist was born, then that moment was when he joined the Shelleys at their house, High Elms, at Bracknell. Once there, he was only a stone's throw from his own Headlong Halls and Nightmare Abbeys.

CHAPTER II

THE SHELLEY PERIOD

THE society in which Peacock found himself when he visited the Shelleys at Bracknell is described in his own words:

At Bracknell, Shelley was surrounded by a numerous society, all in a great measure of his own opinions in relation to religion and politics, and the larger portion of them in relation to vegetable diet. But they wore their rue with a difference. Every one of them adopting some of the articles of the faith of their general church, had each nevertheless some predominant crotchet of his or her own, which left a number of open questions for earnest and not always temperate discussion. I was sometimes irreverent enough to laugh at the fervour with which opinions utterly unconducive to any practical result were battled for as matters of the highest importance to the well-being of mankind; Harriet Shelley was always ready to laugh with me, and we thereby lost caste with some of the more hot-headed of the party.

The Newtons and the Boinvilles were the chief members of this set, consisting—in Hogg's words—of "two or three sentimental young butchers, an eminently philosophical tinker, and several very unsophisticated medical practitioners"; and they disliked Peacock and were anxious to keep Shelley away from him. This, at least, is true of the women, for with Newton himself Peacock appears to have been on good terms then and later. It was this Newton who was afterwards caricatured or (for he was fantastic enough) portrayed as Mr. Toobad in *Nightmare Abbey,* and Peacock's account of him is interesting.

He was an estimable man and an agreeable companion, and he was not the less amusing that he was the absolute impersonation of a single theory, or rather of two single theories rolled into one. He held that all diseases and all aberrations, moral and physical, had their origin in the use of animal food and of fermented and spirituous liquors; that the universal adoption of a diet of roots, fruits, and distilled water, would restore the golden age of universal health, purity, and peace; that this most ancient and sublime morality was mystically inculcated in the most ancient Zodiac, which was that of Dendera; that this Zodiac was divided into two hemispheres, the upper hemisphere being the realm of Oromazes or the principle of good, the lower that of Ahrimanes or the principle of evil; that each of these hemispheres was again divided into two compartments, and that the four lines of division radiating from the centre were the prototype of the Christian cross.

We are told that Newton saw the Zodiac in everything. Once when he and Peacock were out for a walk, they came on a public-house that had the sign of four horse-shoes. Newton was immediately convinced that this was a representation, from remote antiquity, of the four compartments of the Zodiac. He went inside to ask the landlord if this sign had always four horse-shoes, and was told that usually it was four, though three were not unknown. "I cannot divide the Zodiac into three," Newton remarked. "But it is mostly four. Do you know why it is mostly four?" "Why, sir," the landlord replied, "I suppose because a horse has four legs." Whereupon, Newton bounced out in great indignation and cried to Peacock: "Did you ever see such a fool?"

The incident might have come directly from a Peacock novel, and in Newton, it is clear, we have a typical Peacock character ready-made. Here at last is Peacock's obvious prey (though not, by any means, his only prey), the crank, with his ubiquitous crotchet, convinced that one thing alone can save the world. But the conventional pseudo-romantic poet in him had not yet entirely given place to the satirist. Although he laughed at Newton and his Bracknell friends from the first, yet he could elaborately plan a long poem, twelve cantos of Spenserian stanzas, based on nothing more than Newton's Zodiacal fancies, and actually finish one canto of it, published after his death as the fragment, *Ahrimanes*. He seems, however, to have been genuinely attracted by the notion of the perpetual battle for the world between Oromazes and Ahrimanes, which formed the subject of the poem, and there are references in their correspondence that suggest that it was a frequent topic in his talks with Shelley. But the satirist, if not the humorist, was now pushing his way forward, and it was probably his emergence that caused the poem to be thrown aside. After his tour in the North with the Shelleys, Peacock returned at the end of 1813 to Chertsey, but was not separated from his new friends, who took a house not far away, at Windsor. During the winter he probably worked away at the two comedies, *The Dilettanti* and *The Three Doctors,* though there is evidence to show that they were begun much earlier. These pieces, crude affairs in which the author shows no sense of the theatre and only gives us a shadow of his own unique virtues, are chiefly interesting because they furnished him with material, characters, situations, speeches, that he afterwards used, and improved upon, in his first novel, and also because they are proof that he reached fiction, which gave him the opportunity he required, by way of the stage, for which, in spite of his genius for dialogue, he had no real aptitude. The change from one form to the other, with the retention of some of the usages of drama in the narrative form, was an admirable move, and the fact that it was made so quickly suggests that Peacock's powers and judgment, after some years of very slow growth, were now rapidly developing.

The satirist finds his way into print early in 1814, when *Sir Proteus, a satirical Ballad,* was published, under the name of P. M. O'Donovan. It has an ironical dedication, too clumsy to be effective, to Lord Byron. There are six parts and a short *envoi* and, as usual, a large number of footnotes, in which there is more sting than in the actual verses. At the end of the first part, after some thrusts at Southey, Proteus is called upon to assume any shape but those "which taste and nature wear". Peacock then proceeds to lay about him, with more appearance of bad temper than wit, among a host of poets and politicians and critical reviewers, the Lake Poets, Jeffrey, Campbell, Scott, being the chief literary victims. The satire is chiefly interesting because it shows by contrast the superiority of the method he later made his own. Just as most of the persons, down to Sir William Curtis and Croker (who ". . . fights his battles o'er, and doubly kills the slain"), so heavily assailed in these verses make their appearance again in the novels, so, too, Peacock uses many of the same thrusts to despatch them, but a comparison between this conventional verse-and-footnote manner of attack and his later method, that of bringing the personages on the stage and making them speak for themselves, is all in favour of the fiction, not only on the score of literary interest but of deadly satirical effect.

In the same month, March 1814, that saw the announcement of *Sir Proteus,* the Shelleys were remarried in Hanover Square, their first marriage having been a Scotch one. A month or two later, Shelley, still in London, was helpless in the grip of a new passion, and sent for Peacock, who found him with bloodshot eyes, disordered hair and dress, and with a bottle of laudanum in his hand. By the end of July he had left the country with Mary Wollstonecraft Godwin. Peacock, who would seem to have urged the claims of Harriet before the separation, remained her friend and partisan, and during the time that Shelley was on the Continent, as we know from a letter that Shelley wrote to his wife (in which Peacock, now out of favour, is called "expensive, inconsiderate and cold" a judgment with which Harriet can hardly have agreed), Peacock looked after Harriet's affairs for him. Later, however, when Shelley returned, Peacock was one of the first, if not the first, of his friends to see him, and during the following winter, when Peacock was apparently living with his mother in Southampton Buildings, Chancery Lane, both he and Shelley were able to help one another to escape from their respective creditors. By the summer of 1815 Peacock had left London for Marlow and Shelley had taken a house at

Bishopsgate, so that they were now only a short distance from one another. They went walking together very frequently, and on one occasion, accompanied by Mary Godwin and Charles Clairmont, they set out on a voyage of exploration up the Thames and went as far as Lechlade, in Gloucestershire. It was on this expedition, at Oxford, to be precise, that Peacock told Shelley, who was in bad health, to substitute for his customary diet of tea and lemonade and bread-and-butter "Three mutton chops, well peppered". Clairmont records that he liked Peacock, "an idly-inclined man", not happy unless he was out in summer from morning till night, and that he would have liked him still more "if Shelley had not prejudiced me". This prejudice did nothing to interrupt the companionship of Shelley and Peacock during the summer and winter of 1815, when they read Greek together, sailed their paper boats, and walked and argued without ceasing. It may have been due to some momentary difference or some lurking resentment of Peacock's championship of Harriet, which did not endear him to Mary. It was not until years had passed that Mary Shelley discovered that there was something to be said for Peacock's point of view.

His attitude towards this famous affair may seem puzzling at first, if only because he contrived to remain friendly with all parties. It has been explained by some Shelley enthusiasts, who do not allow their admiration for his doctrine of universal love to lure them into any foolish charity towards his associates, by the simple process of turning Peacock into a cynical sponger, not courageous enough openly to take Shelley's part, nor yet honest enough to deny himself his share of the Shelley spoil. This is unfair, particularly so because there is in it the deceitful shadow of truth. There was perhaps a grain of cynicism, as distinct from humorous scepticism, in Peacock's attitude towards Shelley and his affairs. Peacock could readily take sides on any question, but he had not the temperament of a thorough-going partisan. Nor was he likely, at this or any other time, to find his way into that state of high moral indignation concerning other people's private problems which is so accessible to so many persons. There is no reason to suppose that his attitude had changed during the forty odd years that elapsed between these events and the composition of his *Memoirs* of Shelley, and, in spite of a certain reserve, he makes that attitude clear in those memoirs. He liked Harriet and gives us (as he also did in *Nightmare Abbey*) a very pleasing picture of her, ending with the words: "She was fond of her husband, and accommodated herself in every way to his tastes. If they mixed in society, she adorned it; if they lived in retirement, she was satisfied; if they travelled, she enjoyed the change of scene". Her conduct as a wife, he declares emphatically, "was as pure, as true, as absolutely faultless, as that of any who for such conduct are held most in honour". He points out that the separation took place not after long estrangement, not by mutual consent, but simply by reason of the fact that Shelley could not withstand the onslaught of his new passion for Mary Godwin, whose "great personal and intellectual attractions" Peacock readily admits. He also admits that "Shelley's second wife was intellectually better suited to him than the first", and points out that Shelley stood more in need of this kind of

sympathy than most men. After receiving the con-
fidences of both his friends, the distracted husband and
the injured wife, it was impossible for Peacock, as it
would be for any sensible person so situated, to take
a side, even if he had been by nature an out-and-out
partisan. He allows Shelley to escape without con-
demnation, only protesting against any attempt to throw
the blame upon Harriet. Living with the events,
he saw them for what they were, a tangled piece of
tragi-comedy and not a cut-and-dried problem in ethics.
But though he saw no reason why he should either
condemn Shelley or libel Harriet, that does not mean
that he had no opinion whatsoever on the transac-
tion. Reading between the lines of his very guarded
Memoir (with particular attention to the references to
Southey), we can see that he still held the view he must
have expressed more than once during the summer of
1814, that the separation and the subsequent elopement
were a mistake, causing unnecessary suffering to all the
people concerned, and that Shelley would have been
wiser if he had given his passion time to cool and had
remained by the side of his wife. This opinion would
be strengthened by another opinion, though of this we
have no direct evidence. It is significant, however,
that while Peacock's references to Mary are scrupu-
lously fair, those to Harriet are positively enthusiastic,
and we may take leave to father upon him the opinion
that Harriet would ultimately have made Shelley the
better wife of the two. Shelley, in Peacock's opinion,
needed balance even more than he needed intellectual
sympathy, and Harriett, who had laughed with Peacock
at Bracknell, who had common sense and a sprightly
humour as opposed to Mary's enthusiasm and ardent

sympathy, was in a far better position to restore this balance.

Meanwhile, this friendship grew with the passing months. The record of it is largely a record of summer excursions and winter studies, varied by occasional visits to London, where they attended the play or the opera or spent the evening in talk with Hunt or Godwin. By this time Peacock was receiving a small annuity from Shelley, and in return he made himself useful in various ways. When Shelley was in Switzerland, during the summer of 1816, Peacock acted as his agent in Harriet's affairs and was commissioned to find a house for him. In December, when Harriet committed suicide, Shelley immediately consulted Peacock, who advised him to marry Mary Godwin at once. After the marriage, which took place at the end of the year, the Shelleys became his neighbours at Marlow and entered upon the happiest year of their friendship. "This was an agreeable year to all of us," Peacock writes. "Mr. Hogg was a frequent visitor. We had a good deal of rowing and sailing, and we took long walks in all directions." Evidence of their close companionship is furnished by one of Mrs. Shelley's letters: "Peacock dines here every day, *uninvited*, to drink his bottle. I have not seen him; he morally disgusts me; and Marianne (Mrs. Hunt) says that he is very ill-tempered", a passage that suggests that either Mrs. Shelley was still prejudiced against the friend of Harriet or that his sardonic humour, now rapidly maturing, was not to the taste of these ladies. Indeed, Peacock could never be called a ladies' man at this or any other time of his life, but he appears to have been always sufficiently popular with men, who found him a good companion in his youth and a great original in his old age.

Headlong Hall, Peacock's first novel, was written during 1815 and published at the very end of that year. A notice in *The Critical Review* called the author a "laughing philosopher", a description that was applied to him for the rest of his life; but the novel attracted little attention in the Reviews. A second edition, however, was published about the middle of the following year, and there is evidence that the book was soon widely known in literary circles. This is not the place for literary criticism of this and the succeeding novels, which will be examined in detail in a later chapter. Peacock's novels of opinion can be regarded either as pieces of comic fiction, that is, as works of art, or as pieces of topical satire, in which certain contemporary doctrines and persons, political, literary, and so forth, are ridiculed. There are really two men at work in these novels: one is a humorist, expressing a universal mockery, laughing at life itself; the other is a satirist, a man who wrote only for his contemporaries and with the purpose of advancing one set of opinions and denouncing, if only indirectly, another set of opinions. That the two cannot in the last resort be separated is no reason why, for purposes of convenience, we should not make some sort of division between them. (Indeed, Peacock has suffered because critics have found it easier to deal with the satirist than the humorist.) Here, in this chronicle of his life, it will be more convenient to examine each succeeding novel only in its more superficial aspect as a work of topical satire, giving a key to the characters and the situations and so forth, without attempting any estimate or analysis of them as pieces of literature. That can very well come later, when there will be ample space for it, and it will be no bad thing for Peacock if, for once, criticism does not expend all its energy on the topical satire but reserves some of it for an account of those qualities in his work that have a comparatively universal appeal.

In *Headlong Hall* Peacock first made use of the scheme that afterwards he put to such good uses. Squire Headlong, who has a thirst for knowledge as well as for liquor, invites a company of learned persons to stay with him in Wales. Once there, these persons argue and dine and join in choruses and, finally, the younger members of the party marry themselves off with surprising celerity. The chief characters, Mr. Foster, the perfectibilarian, Mr. Escot, the deteriorationist, and Mr. Jenkinson, the statu-quo-ite, who argue for and against progress throughout the novel, probably owe their existence to the talks that had so often taken place between Shelley, Peacock and Hogg, but Peacock made no attempt to put himself and his two friends on the stage of his comedy, but only created mouthpieces for three familiar points of view. The introduction of Mr. Cranium is a hit at the passing enthusiasm for phrenology, which had just received serious attention from the *Edinburgh Review*. This is probably the review that is attacked and ridiculed in the personages of its editor and contributors, Messrs. Gall, Treacle, MacLaurel and Nightshade, who may be taken to represent (leaving out Treacle, who is probably nobody in particular), Jeffrey, Campbell and Southey. Mr. Panscope, the obscure all-round philosopher, is Peacock's first, and worst, attempt at Coleridge. Miss Philomela Poppyseed, the novelist with whom the reviewers are on such good terms, is Mrs. Amelia Opie, whose kindly treatment by the *Edinburgh* was the subject of a footnote to *Sir Proteus.* The identification of all these literary characters is rather uncertain and a matter of no importance, if only because the satire with which they are concerned is very general. Dr. Gaster is the first of Peacock's gourmandising parsons, but is unlike some of the later ones, who are ripe scholars, in being a mere ignorant glutton. One of Peacock's few romantic traits was his love of wild scenery and natural luxuriance of landscape in every form, so that it is not to be wondered at that he detested the formal landscape gardening much in vogue during this time. One of the most celebrated and most pompous professors of this bastard art was Humphrey Repton, whom Peacock had caricatured in one of his comedies as Mr. Milestone. He reappears, of course, in *Headlong Hall,* and some of its most entertaining passages are based on Repton's controversies with Sir Uvedale Price (now Sir Patrick O'Prism) and Payne Knight, the author of *The Landscape,* who does not appear himself but whose point of view is enforced by Peacock. For the most part, however, the satire in *Headlong Hall* is very general, more so than that in any of the other novels of opinion, and gives the reader little more than a hint of the author's own attitude towards the various subjects under discussion. It may be said to be a preliminary skirmish with the Crotchet.

Towards the end of 1816, Shelley wrote to Leigh Hunt:

Peacock is the author of *Headlong Hall,*—he expresses himself much pleased by your approbation—indeed it is an approbation which many would be happy to acquire! He is now writing *Melincourt* in the same style, but, as I judge, far superior to *Headlong Hall*. He is an amiable man of great learning, considerable taste, an enemy to every shape of tyranny and superstitious imposture.

The reference to the authorship of *Headlong Hall* was necessary because the book was published anonymously. Its successor appeared either in February or March 1817 in three volumes. *The British Critic,* detecting in the work "the cloven foot of infidelity", abused it at length and so foolishly as to justify the author's most extravagant satire of the reactionary reviewers. The novel was much admired, however, in the Liberal camp, found its way to America, and was translated into French. It was even imitated before the year was out. Shelley regarded it as Peacock's best tale, and was never tired of singing its praises. That *Melincourt* is "in the same style" as *Headlong Hall,* though much longer (it is the longest of all Peacock's novels) and more varied, is true enough. There is the same scheme, the same assemblage, though now in more than one place, of crotcheteers, and the author displays the same contempt for the ordinary usages of fiction, openly quoting the more absurd remarks of the people he caricatures, blandly inserting footnotes that refer the reader to his authorities. In some other respects, however, *Melincourt* is quite unlike Peacock's first novel, and it is this difference, due to a change in the attitude of the author himself, that explains Shelley's partiality, his belief that it was "far superior" because it was "more serious".

In *Headlong Hall* it is difficult to detect the author's own point of view. Now, in *Melincourt,* there is no mistaking it. Of all Peacock's novels it is the most definitely satirical in intention and the most topical. That is why from being the most admired of all his novels it has gradually come to be the least admired, for it may be said to have lost force with every succeeding year since its first appearance. Instead of mocking the crotchet in general, Peacock now takes a side. Openly declaring himself to be of one party, he proceeds to attack the other. This explains why the two chief characters, Mr. Forester, the naturalistic reformer (in whom there is a good deal of Shelley, whose influence is apparent throughout), and his Anthelia are merely prigs, and why their talk makes up the dullest chapters Peacock ever wrote. They are there to represent a point of view that is meant to be seriously accepted, and for this method of approach Peacock had not the right kind of imagination. On the other hand, most of the satire, being immediately topical and there for a definite purpose, is single-edged and not, like so much of Peacock's satire, double-edged. (A notable exception, however, is that which circles about the figure of Sir Oran Haut-ton, perhaps the best character in the book, although he never utters a word.) There are one or two minor crotcheteers, such as Mr. Derrydown, the ballad-enthusiast, but most of the characters are introduced to ridicule and discredit what Peacock imagined to be the forces of reaction, literary, political and social, of his time. For the most part, these characters must be regarded as a rough personification of the views of actual individuals, and not, as is frequently supposed, caricatures of the persons themselves. We are at liberty to identify Feathernest with Southey, Mystic with Coleridge, Paperstamp with Wordsworth,

Vamp with Gifford, Anyside Antijack with Canning, Mr. Fax with Malthus (whose prominent part and gentle treatment are rather curious), Mr. Killthedead with Croker, but we must not imagine that Peacock thought he was portraying these gentlemen. All that he was doing, as we shall presently see when we come to consider his methods more closely, was creating fantastic personages out of their opinions. His real quarry throughout this book is the *Quarterly Review* type of mind. Thus, the great scene at Mainchance Villa is simply a brilliant and impudent dramatisation of a *Quarterly* article against parliamentary reform. The best chapters in the whole book, those describing the election at Onevote, are nothing more than the customary arguments for reform, of the kind that Shelley himself had used in a pamphlet, put into dramatic shape, turned into roaring but stinging farce. Ironically enough, this satirist of the crotchet has now become a crotcheteer himself, as the frequent references to West Indian sugar and paper money throughout the story amply testify. The Cimmerian Lodge episode, too, had obviously nothing to do with party affairs, but is Peacock's own protest against what he takes to be the wilful obscurity of Coleridge and his admired German philosophers. The satire, however, is too savage and clumsy to be very effective, and here, as elsewhere in *Melincourt,* the author is obviously laying about him too hastily, attacking before he has had time to discover his opponent's weak places, heavily trampling down men of straw.

Throughout 1817 Shelley and Peacock had been working away, side by side, at long narrative poems, which made their appearance, as *The Revolt of Islam* and

Rhododaphne, early in 1818. Like most of Peacock's
work, *Rhododaphne* was published anonymously, and
though its authorship seems to have been an open secret
in London, where at least one review announced that
it was "from the pen of Mr. Peacock", this anonymity
led to confusion. In America, for example, where the
poem was soon reprinted and later numbered Poe among
its admirers, it was for years regarded as the work
of a Virginian poet. It is the longest and most ambitious
of Peacock's poems and, if we except certain lyrics,
easily the most successful. In its own day it was greatly
admired. Byron patted the "Grecian Enchantress" on
the head. Shelley wrote an enthusiastic review, unfortunately never printed, in which he cried: "This it is to
be a scholar; this it is to have read Homer and Sophocles
and Plato!" There is certainly an enthusiastic scholar,
master of classical allusion and charming fancy, even
if not a born poet, behind this narrative, filled with
bright clear imagery, of the loves of Anthemion and
Calliroë and Rhododaphne, against a background of
Thessalian magic, the spoil of many journeys with that
Golden Ass. Here his passion for the antique world,
which leads him merely to make sardonic contrasts
in his prose satire, comes to fruition, and there is a
genuine ring in that passage of regret at the beginning of the third canto, that passage ending with the
lines:

> great Pan is dead:
> The life, the intellectual soul
> Of vale, and grove, and stream, has fled
> For ever with the creed sublime
> That nursed the Muse of earlier time.

Peacock's Hellenic enthusiasm never waned, but it

was during this period that it had most influence upon
his work. He planned a companion poem to *Rhododaphne,* the "nympholeptic tale" to which Shelley refers
in a letter, and of which an elaborate prose abstract,
with references to various authorities and evidence of
the good scholar rather than the rapt poet, was discovered among his papers. It would seem to have been
set aside at the advent of more entertaining or more
urgent work and then finally abandoned in 1821, when
Horace Smith's *Amarynthus the Nympholept* was published. To this period, too, we can assign the fragment *Calidore,* a tale that had borrowed material from
an early, perhaps the earliest, attempt at narrative, a
tiny fragment called *Satyrane; or, The Stranger in
England.* It is this basic idea, the familiar satiric
device of the visiting stranger, that is taken over in
Calidore, an ironic fantasy of the type beloved by
Anatole France. It is a considerable fragment, but
unfortunately not continuous. One part describes the
adventures of a godlike youth, Calidore, who has been
the companion of Greek gods and Arthurian heroes,
and who lands in Wales and promptly falls in love.
He spends a Peacockian evening at an inn. Another
part describes the arrival of King Arthur, Gwenevere,
Merlin, and Sir Launcelot and their friends at an island,
where they meet Bacchus and Pan and are told that
this is the place chosen by the old gods for their
dwelling-place during their exile from the world of
men. The Arthurian company decides to remain there,
and it is quite evident that Calidore is its representative,
whose duty it is to report on the condition of England.
Another fragment shows him in London and gives
Peacock an opportunity for indulging one of his own

crotchets, his dislike for paper-money. The scheme of *Calidore* is far more complicated and ambitious than any of Peacock's completed tales, and this may possibly explain why it was never finished, for Peacock was anything but a plotter, his inventive powers were feeble, and it is more than likely that while he found it easy enough to sketch in a few detached scenes, the task of stitching together the whole fabric of narrative proved to be too much for his powers or his patience.

Meanwhile, his days of companionship with Shelley were numbered. The beginning of 1818 found them all studying Italian together, for now Shelley had decided to leave for Italy as soon as possible. The time before the actual embarkation was spent in London, when the Shelleys, with Peacock and Hogg in constant attendance, were much in company, Godwin, Leigh Hunt, Keats, Novello and Charles Lamb being among their visitors. On the very last evening, March 10, Peacock, as he is careful to tell us, attended the first performance of Rossini's *Barbiere di Siviglia* and then went round to Shelley's lodgings close by and had supper with the travellers. Before the guests had gone, Shelley fell asleep and so they crept out without waking him. Early next morning he was gone, and Peacock never saw him again.

Letters between them, however, were fairly frequent and the early ones throw a light upon their respective activities. Thus, writing from Milan in April, Shelley makes a reference to *Nightmare Abbey,* which must have been begun before he left England, and several weeks later, Peacock replies:

I have almost finished *Nightmare Abbey.* I think it necessary to "make a stand" against the "encroachments" of black bile. The fourth canto of *Childe Harold* is really too bad. I cannot consent to be *auditor tantum* of this systematical "poisoning" of the "mind" of the "reading public".

These remarks are valuable not only because they "date" the story but also because they show us in what light the author regarded it. There was, however, some delay, for the novel was not published until the following November, when it attracted surprisingly little attention. Ironically enough, when we consider that the tale is frequently held to be an act of treachery on Peacock's part, the most enthusiastic contemporary reference to it is from none other than the victim himself. Shelley did not receive a copy until June 1819, when he immediately wrote:

I am delighted with *Nightmare Abbey*. I think Scythrop a character admirably conceived and executed; and I know not how to praise sufficiently the lightness, chastity, and strength of the language of the whole. It perhaps exceeds all your works in this. The catastrophe is excellent. I suppose the moral is contained in what Falstaff says: "For God's sake, talk like a man of this world"; and yet, looking deeper into it, is not the misdirected enthusiasm of Scythrop what J. C. calls the "salt of the earth"? My friends the Gisbornes here admire and delight in it exceedingly.

What Peacock did in *Nightmare Abbey* was to take the situation in which Shelley found himself in the summer of 1814 and exploit it for purposes of satire and comedy. The central figure of the book, Scythrop Glowry is deliberately made unlike Shelley in many details, but is certainly intended as a caricature of one side of the poet's mind, is a creature formed out of his opinions, and was accepted as such by Shelley himself, who showed no resentment. The two girls with whom

Scythrop finds himself in love are undoubtedly taken from Shelley's history. The first, Marionetta O'Carroll, is Harriet Shelley even to certain physical details, as will readily be seen when Peacock's description of Harriet in his *Memoirs* is compared with the description of Marionetta in the story. The second, Stella, is described as being as far removed as possible in appearance from Mary Shelley, but she has the same temperament and outlook, and her appeal to Scythrop is precisely that of Mary to Shelley in 1814. After that, however, apart from a few touches here and there, all likeness to Shelley's actual history ends, for all Scythrop's farcical adventures, which conclude with his losing both ladies and consoling himself with Madeira, belong to fiction. Not a few critics have been unjust to this novel and its author because their own interests have led them to exaggerate the importance of the part that Shelley's story plays in Peacock's comedy. They write as if *Nightmare Abbey* had been created merely in order to ridicule the poet's most intimate affairs, whereas the truth is that Peacock made use of those affairs only so far as they assisted his main purpose, with which Shelley had little or nothing to do. So, too, they would frequently seem to suggest that Peacock is simply making what capital he can out of a famous chapter in his friend's life, and obviously overlook the fact that at the time when *Nightmare Abbey* appeared Shelley's affairs were not matters of general public concern, were indeed only known to a few. All that Peacock wanted was to find a situation that would serve as the basis of a satirical novel, and his memory of the events of four years before provided him with one, which was fortunate because his inventive powers were feeble. Given such a situation, with the chief personages ready to hand, he was soon able to work it up into a brilliant satirical comedy.

What his chief purpose was is perfectly obvious after the most casual reading of *Nightmare Abbey*, but if there should still be any doubt, his own references to the book will settle the question. We have already seen that he can write, in connection with it, of the necessity of making a stand "against the encroachments of black bile". Writing again to Shelley, later, he says:

I thought I had fully explained to you the object of *Nightmare Abbey*, which was to bring into philosophical focus a few of the morbidities of modern literature, and to let in a little daylight on its atrabilarious complexion.

His prey now is contemporary ultra-romaniticism, those "blue devils" that keep popping up in the book, just as before, in *Melincourt*, it was reactionary sentiment. The romantic poets and German philosophers have now taken the place of *Quarterly* reviewers. During the surprisingly short interval between the two books, Peacock's mind has swung round, and he is now no longer the radical advocate, turning Shelley into the solemn Mr. Forester, but the spokesman of cheerful common sense, transforming Shelley, but an earlier and more grotesquely romantic Shelley, into the moping Scythrop. Nearly all the other characters are there because of their association with the "blue devils". Coleridge reappears once more, this time in a more recognisable shape, as Mr. Flosky, who is more sympathetically treated than the Mr. Panscope of *Headlong Hall* or the Mr. Mystic of *Melincourt* but is really a far more deadly caricature. Mr. Flosky's talk, particularly his diverting dialogue with Marionetta, who applies to him in vain for a

simple piece of information, is really a very shrewd
thrust at the pompous and rather silly side of Coleridge's metaphysical criticism and lay sermonising. He
takes his place in the book as the mystery-monger-in-
chief. Mr. Cypress, who makes a brief but very
successful appearance, is of course Byron, who is compelled to paraphrase his elaborate lamentations in *Childe
Harold* into pithy prose and thereby make them sound
very foolish. His song, "There is a fever of the
spirit", is a marvellous *pastiche* of the Byronic manner. Mr. Toobad, who believed that the world is
alternately governed by powers of light and darkness and that this is the age of darkness, the reign
of Ahrimanes, is our old Bracknell friend, J. F.
Newton, who, it is said, delighted in repeating such
phrases as "the devil is come among you having
great wrath" though it is hardly likely that he
repeated them so often and with such droll effect as
Mr. Toobad does. Mr. Listless is a grotesque sketch
of the well-known contemporary dandy, Sir Lumley
Skeffington, with whom Peacock had probably come
into contact through Shelley. The other characters
are merely general types. Mr. Asterias, who devotes
his life to the task of finding "the orang-outangs
of the sea", is simply a specimen of the industrious
but silly scientist who was then beginning to make his
appearance. Mr. Larynx is the inevitable parson,
always on hand to finish a bottle or join in a chorus.
Mr. Glowry is pessimism itself, and, in opposition
to him and to the whole set, is Mr. Hilary, who
represents cheerful common sense and is largely Peacock's own mouthpiece. With these characters and
the farcical business he contrived out of Shelley's

affair, Peacock built up what is easily the most brilliant and deftly-shaped and satisfying of the three novels he had written so far, a story that shows him developing now very rapidly as satirist and humorist and literary craftsman. In spite of its cool reception *Nightmare Abbey* soon became one of the most popular of all his works.

During the year that saw the departure of Shelley and the publication of *Nightmare Abbey,* one period of Peacock's life may be said to end, and before beginning a new chapter with an account of his new activities, we will go forward a little in time and conclude this chapter of his life with Shelley by following their friendship to its conclusion. They corresponded irregularly, but at considerable length. Peacock acted more or less as Shelley's literary agent in London, reading proofs and seeing publishers. When the poet was meditating *The Cenci,* he sent Peacock a translation of the original story and demanded his opinion as to whether it was suitable for the stage, and though this opinion was unfavourable, later, when the play was finished, Peacock was presented with the hopeless task of persuading the theatrical managers to produce it. *Prometheus Unbound* was also sent on to Peacock before publication, and he it was who saw it, not very successfully, through the press. Shelley's famous *Defence of Poetry* was written as a reply to Peacock's deliberately provocative *Four Ages of Poetry,* and in its original form contained a number of friendly allusions to Peacock and his essay. These allusions were removed by John Hunt, who had accepted the essay for *The Liberal,* which did not, however, live long enough to print it, and they were not replaced because Mrs. Shelley afterwards made use of Hunt's copy. During this same year, 1821, Shelley, who was very depressed and wished he had "something better to do than furnish this jingling food for oblivion, called verse" (though this phrase occurs in a later letter), "expressed a wish to be employed politically at the court of a native prince"; and Peacock was compelled to discourage him, pointing out that such a position in India would agree with neither his mind nor his body, and that anyhow it could not be obtained for him because the Indian Civil Service was restricted to the covenanted servants of the Company. He approved, however, of the notion, wished to see Shelley "following some scheme of flesh and blood, some interesting matter connected with the business of life", and promised to make a diligent search for something suitable. It is possible that this search might have been successful and that for a short time, a very short time, we might have had a merchanting or brokering Shelley, had it been prosecuted a little longer. But July 1822 brought its tragedy. For some time Peacock had been attending to his friend's tangled affairs, and now he was appointed joint executor with Byron of his will. He received a legacy of £500, and an additional £2000 for an annuity. This was handsome but by no means unearned, for all the work fell upon him and it was he who conducted the various negotiations between Mrs. Shelley and her father-in-law, and there is ample evidence, in spite of Mrs. Shelley's complaints about lost boxes and the like, that he performed the work like the excellent man of business he was. Thus ended one of the most curious friendships in the history of English Letters.

CHAPTER III

In the summer of 1818 Peacock and his mother settled
in a new house at Marlow. Here he spent the last few
months of his liberty, and, as we learn from a diary
that he kept for a short time, he spent them in the old
way, writing a little (mostly an *Essay on Fashionable
Literature,* which was never finished and is chiefly interesting because it praises such writers as Wordsworth,
Coleridge and Scott), reading a great deal, and making
daily excursions either afoot or on the river. We do
not know exactly why this summer should have put
an end to his easy independent life. It may be that
the family means had been gradually reduced, though it
is more likely that Peacock himself, some time during
this year, suffered a heavy loss. Indeed, there is a tradition that he backed a bill, or otherwise went security,
for a friend, Peter Auber, and met disaster that way.
Whatever the cause, he was now anxious to make
money and find some regular employment, and for a time
considered the possibility of a new liberal review. In
the autumn, however, there came an opportunity he
could not afford to miss. It had been decided to recon-
struct the Examiner's Department of the East India
Company, and Auber, who was the Deputy-Secretary,
told Peacock that there would soon be a vacancy in

that office. Peacock had first to prepare a paper on Indian affairs for the Committee of Correspondence. At the beginning of 1819 he went up to London, living with his mother at York Street, Covent Garden, and attended every day at the India House for six weeks, during which time he was called upon to pass an examination. This he did with complete success, his papers being marked "Nothing superfluous, and nothing wanting" (which might serve as an excellent description of his prose style), and in May he was appointed Assistant to the Examiner at a salary of £600. There were three others, Edward Strachey, James Mill, the philosopher, and J. J. Harcourt. All four were on probation for two years, at the end of which time their appointments were confirmed and their salaries increased by £200. Peacock now became the man of affairs from ten to four, and was chaffed by his literary associates (as Leigh Hunt told Shelley) for "his new Oriental grandeur, his Brahminical learning, and his inevitable tendencies to be one of the corrupt". The middle of the summer saw him comfortably settled, with his mother, at 18 Stamford Street, Blackfriars.

Having now an assured income and a house, he bethought him of a wife. He had been friendly for years with a certain Marianne, whose name occasionally crops up in his letters over a long period, and there was some talk of his marrying her. (Mrs. Leigh Hunt was a Marianne too, but it is easy to see which is meant in the correspondence.) But nothing came of the friendship and we do not even know who she was. In November 1819 he set about obtaining a wife in a very Peacockian and philosophical fashion. Not since

1811 had he seen Jane Gryffydh or communicated with her, but now, just as if he were one of his own characters and the story was nearing the end, he coolly made her an offer of marriage by letter. His astonishing proposal ran as follows:

It is more than eight years since I had the happiness of seeing you: I can scarcely hope that you have remembered me as I have remembered you; yet I feel confident that the simplicity and ingenuousness of your disposition will prompt you to answer me with the same candor with which I write to you. I long entertained the hopes of returning to Merionethshire under better auspices than those under which I left it: but fortune always disappointed me, continually offering me prospects which receded as I approached them. Recently she has made amends for her past unkindness, and has given me much present good, and much promise of progressive prosperity, which leaves me nothing to desire in worldly advantage, but to participate it with you. The greatest blessing this world could bestow on me would be to make you my wife: consider if your own feelings would allow you to constitute my happiness. I desire only to promote yours; and I desire only you: for your value is beyond fortune, of which I want no more than I have. The same circumstances which have given me prosperity confine me to London, and to the duties of the department with which the East India Company has entrusted me: yet I can absent myself for a few days once in every year: if you sanction my wishes, with what delight should I employ them in bringing you to my home! If this be but a baseless dream: if I am even no more in your estimation than the sands on the seashore—yet I am sure, as I have already said, that you will answer me with the same candor with which I have written. Whatever may be your sentiments, the feelings with which I now write to you, and which more than eight years of absence and silence have neither obliterated nor diminished, will convince you that I never can be otherwise than most sincerely and affectionately your friend.

It is dated from East India House, which suggests, as a final touch of absurdity, that it was written during office hours. When we consider the awkwardness of the situation, however, we must agree that this is a very able document, promising much for the future Assistant-Examiner. The suggested picture of himself as a man who has grappled with fortune for years and at last found his efforts rewarded, is nicely calculated to arouse feminine sympathy, far more so than any account of himself as we have actually seen him, happily idling for years and then luckily falling into a snug berth just when he really needed one. The letter was completely successful, and five months later Peacock was able to absent himself for a few days and marry his Jane in the Chapel of Eglwysfach in Cardiganshire, returning with her immediately to London. On this strange courtship and marriage, Shelley, writing from Pisa, says the last word:

I congratulate you most sincerely on your choice and on your marriage. . . . I was very much amused by your laconic account of the affair. It is altogether extremely like the *dénouement* of one of your own novels. . . .

His married life was extremely happy, if not altogether fortunate. We do not know very much about Mrs. Peacock, "the milk-white Snowdonian Antelope" as Shelley calls her in his letter to Maria Gisborne, but the few descriptions we have of her in her youth, telling us she was tall and handsome, with fine eyes, simple and direct and with a taste for books, suggest the kind of woman with whom Peacock could be very happy. Their eldest child, Mary Ellen, was born in July 1821; then came a second daughter, Margaret, two years later; and afterwards two more children, a son, Edward

Gryffydh, and another daughter. The last two were not born in London, however, but at Lower Halliford, where Peacock first took a cottage for his mother and then made a home for the whole family by joining another to it. There, at Lower Halliford, he stayed to the end of his life, though for some years he made a practice of remaining in London from Monday morning to Friday evening. They had not been long settled at Halliford when Margaret, the second child, died very suddenly just when she was apparently recovering from an illness and when her father, happy to find her better, was out walking with a friend. The child had been a favourite with both her parents, and the loss in these circumstances was a peculiarly bitter one. It was for her tombstone at Shepperton that Peacock wrote the most moving of all his poems, "Long night succeeds thy little day". His wife suffered intensely from this loss, and not long afterwards began to break down in health, finally becoming a complete invalid. It was owing to her resemblance to the vanished Margaret that the Peacocks adopted a neighbouring child, named Mary Rosewell, who remained under Peacock's roof for the rest of his life.

His work at the East India Office brought him a certain number of new friends. Edward Strachey, Horace Grant and Henry Cole, all colleagues of his, joined a little friendly circle, of which Hogg, Horace Smith and Walter Coulson, editor of *The Globe* from 1822, were also members. He saw a good deal of James Mill and John Stuart Mill, with whom he worked for many years, but never became so friendly with them as he did with some of his other colleagues.

It was not so much difference of opinion (there was more than a little philosophical Radicalism in Peacock, who, incidentally, contrived to make a weekly dining companion of Jeremy Bentham) as difference of tastes and temperament that held them apart. The Mills were not sufficiently expansive and genial for Peacock, who liked mellow companions, scholarly wits, at the board of an evening. Having met the elder Mill for the first time, Coulson remarked to Peacock: "When I know Mill well, shall I like him—will he like what I like and hate what I hate?", and received from Peacock the characteristic reply: "No, he will hate what you hate and hate everything you like". Moreover, Peacock's contempt for the new science of political economy, of which the two Mills were among the most solemn professors, did nothing to increase his regard for them. John Stuart Mill, he told a young friend in 1824, belonged to "a *disquisition* set of young men", and ever afterwards Peacock regarded Mill's philosophical activities and mounting reputation with a very cool sceptical eye. A more congenial acquaintance was Thomas Taylor, the Platonist (who makes a brief appearance in *Melincourt*) a solitary and passionate Greek scholar, with a contempt for Greek accents and university dons. Such was Taylor's passion for the antique world that he was said to have offered sacrifices to its deities in his house at Walworth. Peacock, who was nearly as thoroughgoing a pagan (though we cannot imagine him offering sacrifices), must have found Taylor's Hellenic enthusiasms and amiable crotcheteering an attractive mixture, and at one time he saw a good deal of the queer old man, who called him "Greeky-Peeky".

Peacock's first literary work of any importance after his India House appointment was his essay on *The Four Ages of Poetry,* published in *Ollier's Literary Miscellany* early in 1820. The fact that this essay produced, as a reply, Shelley's better known and entirely serious *Defence of Poetry* must not lead us into mistaking its character. It is not, as Shelley's essay was, an expression of its author's deepest convictions, and might be described as something between a piece of criticism and a domestic joke, a hit at his friends the poets, a specimen of critical "ragging". The basis of it is a belief, half-serious perhaps and not unconnected with the author's comparative failure as a serious poet and his new appearance as a man of affairs, that the time for poetry had passed with the development of social life and scientific knowledge, an opinion that has been put forward, in all seriousness, by several more recent and more solemn critics. When we consider that this essay was written during a period that has since been recognised as perhaps the greatest age of English Poetry, no further refutation seems necessary, but we may take leave to point out that what poetry primarily expresses are men's emotions, and so long as men have emotions there is room for poetry. The triumphant feelings of the scientist who had succeeded in banishing the last rainbow from the sky would be matter for a poem. Moreover, Peacock, like some succeeding critics who have held this view, clearly misunderstood the nature of the art, which can work with myth and symbol and is not dependent upon ordinary belief. The best poetry about fairies, for example, has not necessarily been the work of men who believed in the actual existence of fairies; indeed, it would not be difficult to prove that such a belief would tend to fetter the poet rather than inspire him. Yet this opinion, that poetry is defeated and finally exiled by knowledge, is not simply nonsense, but one of those dangerous half-truths. It is certainly true that as knowledge increases and social life becomes more intricate, poetry is less and less able to take in the whole of life, as it does in Homer for example, and must inevitably retreat inward, as it were, becoming increasingly subjective and symbolic. Thus it avoids defeat and exile by changing its character. Peacock's trick—for he must not be taken too seriously—is to pretend that it therefore ceases to have any value, as if there were only one real kind of poetry. He is artfully begging the question by thus arriving, as he does, at the conclusion that contemporary poetry is almost worthless only by an argument that is really based on the assumption that it is worthless.

This is his real object, in *The Four Ages of Poetry*, to have a fling at his contemporaries. His reasoning is impudent sophistry—and it is plain to any reader who knows his man that he has his tongue in his cheek —but nevertheless, with his usual acuteness, he does contrive to indicate the weakness of the contemporary romantics.

In the origin of perfection of poetry, all the associations of life were composed of poetical materials. With us it is decidedly the reverse. We know, too, that there are no Dryads in Hydepark nor Naiads in the Regent's-canal. But barbaric manners and supernatural interventions are essential to poetry. Either in the scene, or in the time, or in both, it must be remote from our ordinary perceptions. While the historian and the philosopher are advancing in, and accelerating, the progress of knowledge, the poet is wallowing in the rubbish of departed ignorance, and raking up the ashes of dead savages to find gewgaws and rattles for the grown babies of the age. Mr. Scott digs up the poachers and cattle-stealers of the ancient border. Lord Byron cruises for thieves and pirates on the shores of the Morea and among the Grecian islands. Mr. Southey wades through ponderous volumes of travels and chronicles, from which he carefully selects all that is false, useless, and absurd, as being essentially poetical; and when he has a commonplace book full of monstrosities, strings them into an epic. Mr. Wordsworth picks up village legends from old women and sextons; and Mr. Coleridge, to the valuable information acquired from similar sources, superadds the dreams of crazy theologians and the mysticisms of German metaphysics, and favours the world with visions in verse, in which the quadruple elements of sexton, old woman, Jeremy Taylor, and Emmanuel Kant are harmonised into a delicious poetical compound. Mr. Moore presents us with a Persian, and Mr. Campbell with a Pennsylvanian tale, both formed on the same principle as Mr. Southey's epics, by extracting from a perfunctory and desultory perusal of a collection of voyages and travels all that useful investigation would not seek for and that common sense would reject.

It was obviously for the sake of such delightfully impudent flings as this, a passage that might have come out of one of his novels, that the essay was planned and executed. Here is another of them:

A poet in our times is a semi-barbarian in a civilised community. He lives in the days that are past. His ideas, thoughts, feelings, associations, are all with barbarous manners, obsolete customs, and exploded superstitions. The march of his intellect is like that of a crab, backward. . . . The highest inspirations of poetry are resolvable into three ingredients: the rant of unregulated passion, the whining of exaggerated feeling, and the cant of factitious sentiment: and can therefore serve only to ripen a splendid lunatic like Alexander, a puling driveller like Werter, or a morbid dreamer like Wordsworth.

In order to arrive naturally at these provocative conclusions, Peacock makes use of one of those historical
schemes the very neatness and symmetry of which suggest either intellectual naïveté (of which Peacock can
hardly be accused) or a theorist with his tongue in his
cheek. We are told that the ages of poetry are those
of iron, gold, silver and brass. The poets of the iron
age deal, in rough-and-ready fashion, with the life stir-
ring about them; the poets of the golden age find their
inspiration in the previous age of iron, which they
idealise; the poets of the silver age recast and polish
the poetry of the golden age; the poets of the age of
brass, "by rejecting the polish and learning of the age
of silver, and taking a retrograde strike to the barbar-
isms and crude traditions of the age of iron, profess
to return to nature and in reality bring poetry to its second childhood". In classical poetry, we have the barbaric
iron age; then the golden or Homeric; then the silver
or Virgilian; and lastly the brass, the Nonnic. English poetry has the same rise and fall, from the golden
age of Shakespeare through the silver age of Dryden
and the eighteenth-century poets to the contemporary age
of brass.

It is all very dexterous and quietly impudent. Here
and there, no doubt, the essay reflects its author's
genuine opinions. He probably did think that the
art deteriorated, though not so regularly as his essay
would imply. He was convinced, too, that the taste of
his time was bad, and when we remember the success
of such easy versifiers as Moore and "Barry Corn-
wall" (whose "drivelling doggerel" Peacock singles
out for attack in a letter to Shelley dealing with this
very subject of poetic taste), we can only agree with

him. But he also tilts at men who were anything but mere poetasters, at genuine poets whom we found him praising in his unfinished *Essay on Fashionable Literature,* whom he quotes far more frequently than he does the poets of the previous age. On his own theory, he preferred brass to silver. The truth is that he could never resist the temptation to gibe at the Lake Poets, in spite of the fact that he had at heart a real admiration for their best work. Their complacency, solemnity and mutual admiration, their literary and political theorising, all irritated him, so that they were always too obvious a target to be ignored. It is probably as an attempt to flutter such poetical dovecots that *The Four Ages of Poetry* is best regarded.

Two years later, in April 1822, Peacock's most popular story, *Maid Marian,* was published. We know from references in his letters to Shelley and in the diary he kept at that time that he had been at work on the story during 1818; and now, in a note prefixed to the volume, he informs us that "This little work, with the exception of the last three chapters, was all written in the autumn of 1818". Thus he defends himself in advance against the charge of being influenced by *Ivanhoe,* which had made its appearance a year after Peacock had planned and all but finished his tale of the same period. Whatever *Maid Marian* may be, however, it is obviously not an attempt to write an historical novel in the manner of Scott. The story is a unique mixture of idyllic romance, sheer fooling and Peacockian irony. For his plot Peacock did not go further than the ballads (his authorities were said to be *Robin Hood's Garland,* a collection popular during the previous century, and Ritson's *Robin Hood*), and the incidents of the ballads are simply strung together, with some changing of names, to make up the various episodes of the novel. His Robin Hood is the outlawed Earl of Huntington, his Marian the noble Matilda Fitzwater of Elizabethan romance, and his plot partly follows Munday and Chettle's two plays, *The Downfall* and *The Death, of Robert, Earl of Huntington.* Nor did Peacock go any further than the ballads for his descriptions of life in the twelfth century. He makes no attempt at historical accuracy or an elaborate painting of the medieval scene; his archaic touches are few and slight; and the story is full of anachronisms that are probably quite deliberate. The romance of the story does not lie in the action but in its background, which gives us a forest life as idyllic as that in *As You Like It.* Peacock had a genuine passion for the Windsor Forest he knew so well in his boyhood, and whose enclosure he so bitterly resented, and this passion shines in the background of his comic romance. Curiously enough, as we discover from his paper *The Last Day of Windsor Forest,* Peacock had seen the only Robin Hood of his own time. This was during the years 1814-15, when, owing to a flaw in the Enclosure of Windsor Forest Act, a neighbouring farmer and his men were able to hunt and kill the King's deer in certain still unenclosed parts of the Forest. These men, whose humour it was to call themselves Robin Hood and Little John and Scarlett, were constantly threatened by the authorities, who were powerless, however, in face of the faulty Act, and at last were compelled to bring two regiments of cavalry to drive the deer into the enclosed part of the Forest,

Peacock's delight in the wild forest life and his long resentment of the Enclosure explain the genuine enthusiasm with which he paints his idyllic Sherwood. For the rest, *Maid Marian* is not at all romantic. The action, even though it follows the traditional Robin Hood stories, is farcically rough-and-tumble, and is made the occasion of not a little oblique satire. There is, however, too much mere breaking of heads for modern readers, who do not share the taste of Peacock and most of his contemporaries for farcical violence, and though there are a few passages of real wit and Peacockian high spirits, in the tale, it has been always regarded by Peacock enthusiasts as the weakest and least characteristic of his novels. With the general public, on the other hand, *Maid Marian* has been the first favourite. Its success was not immediate. On its first appearance, the more important reviews did not notice it at all. It happened, however, that Charles Kemble read the story and thought there might be a light opera in it. There is of course a strong operatic flavour throughout *Maid Marian,* many of whose scenes such as that between the Baron, Matilda and the friar in chapter iv., are made up of little more than terse and amusing dialogue and snatches of song. There is, too, something pleasantly theatrical about the background, which gives us the unfading golden summer of the scenic artist and the lime-light man. Lastly, in that Friar Michael who afterwards became Friar Tuck, who has all the best speeches in the story and, indeed, bestrides it like a colossus, we have a character ripe for the stage, and of a kind to make an actor-manager's mouth water. Kemble suggested to J. R. Planché that he should make a libretto out of the story, and Planché, without asking anybody's permission, immediately set to work putting together *Maid Marian; or, The Huntress of Arlingford* out of Peacock's story and some odds and ends from *Ivanhoe* and the old ballads. The music was composed by Bishop.

When the libretto was finished, it was offered to Hookham, the publisher of the story, who very foolishly objected to the opera and threatened proceedings. Peacock himself, to whom Planché had gone after meeting this rebuff, was wiser and not only gave his own permission but also secured his publisher's. After some delay and at least one postponement of the first night, the opera was produced, with lavish scenic effects, probably as a special Christmas entertainment, on December 3, 1822, at Covent Garden, where it ran for twenty-seven nights. Kemble himself played Friar Tuck, whose song, "The bramble, the bramble", was the only one Kemble ever sang on the stage, we are told; though there is a reference by Thackeray to the opera, written nearly twenty years later, that suggests that Kemble sang other songs during the performance. That reference, one of Thackeray's casual but inimitable touches, occurs in *The Great Hoggarty Diamond,* where Bob Swinney, the most independent and roistering of the West Diddlesex clerks, is described as always singing "The bramble, the bramble"—"one of Charles Kemble's songs in *Maid Marian,* a play that was all the rage then, taken from a story-book by one Peacock, a clerk in the India House: and a precious good place he has too". Whether the play was all the rage or not—and a run of twenty-seven nights meant more then than a modern playgoer would imagine—the "story-book", which was always mentioned on the libretto and was noticed for the first time in several periodicals when the opera was produced, greatly gained by this association. It was translated into German in 1823, and into French in 1826, and again in 1855. The opera was also produced in New York in January 1824. Curiously enough, we have no evidence of any immediate wide sale of the book in England, though of its comparative popularity among Peacock's novels there can be no question.

Peacock himself was, of course, an operatic enthusiast, and for a long time he did the Covent Garden notices for *The Globe and Traveller,* his friend Coulson's paper. The only other periodical writing he did during the decade was contributed to the *Westminster Review,* the organ of the Philosophical Radicals. Peacock appears to have associated more or less regularly with practically all the members of this group, the Mills, Bentham, Grote, Austin, Albany Fonblanque, Roebuck, and undoubtedly he professed many Utilitarian doctrines, yet he cannot be considered a member of the group himself. When we find Leigh Hunt, in a preface written in 1832, including Peacock among the Utilitarians, we rub our eyes, remembering the hard knocks he distributed among these drab philosophers and political economists. Yet if he is to be confined to one contemporary party, then this is the party. His attitude towards the questions of the time was certainly nearer to that of the Utilitarians than to that of any other set of men in the kingdom. There is a strong likeness between the Epicureanism he professed and the central Utilitarian doctrine. This is made plain in his first contribution to the *Westminster Review,* which appeared in October 1827. He was given Moore's *Epicurean* to review and discovered in it a mere travesty of real Epicureanism. He gives a sympathetic account of the real doctrine, and the conclusion of this account is particularly significant because it shows Peacock's drift towards Utilitarianism:

Thus Epicurus first taught, that general utility, or as Bentham expresses it, "the greatest happiness of the greatest number", is the legitimate end of philosophy; and it is curious to see the same class of persons decrying the same doctrine as impracticably dry, when the word utility precedes the word pleasure, and as too practicably voluptuous when the word pleasure precedes the word utility.

In Moore's book, Peacock found everything he disliked, bad scholarship, sentimental posturing, a great deal of silly writing. His severity was by no means unjustified, but it is amusing to remark how the classical pedant in Peacock, whose existence was noticed in the first chapter, shows his hand. Peacock is chiefly indignant because Moore has not "left the Athenians alone". It is this trespassing upon sacred ground rather than Moore's ignorance *qua* ignorance that is the crime. "He could have found abundance of playthings for the grown children of society", Peacock grumbles, "without dressing up in false apparel the chief of an Athenian school of Philosophy to play the fool and coxcomb for their entertainment." For the most part, however, he does not adopt the "slashing" method favoured by hostile reviewers of that time: he is very quiet but he is also very deadly. Moore talks about chapels and spires, and Peacock drily demands the Attic word for a chapel, and asks his author to tell him where the

Athenian found his notion of a spire. When Moore writes:

Among solitary columns and sphinxes, already half sunk from sight, Time seemed to stand waiting, till all that now flourished around should fall beneath his desolating hand like the rest. . . .

Peacock remarks:

The sands of the Libyan desert gaining on Memphis like a sea is an impressive though not original image, but the picture is altogether spoiled by the figure of Time standing waiting. Has Mr. Moore forgotten that time and tide wait neither for men nor sands? The very essence of the idea of Time is steady, incessant, interminable progression. If he has any business in the place, it is an agent, himself silently impelling the progress of desolation, not waiting till the sands have done their work, in order to begin his. And as Memphis was still a flourishing city at least four centuries later than our very curious specimen of an Epicurean, Time must have stood waiting for no inconsiderable portion of himself.

It is all very deft and deadly, and must be accounted one of the most witty and shattering reviews of the century.

Peacock would now seem to be almost settled in the Utilitarian camp, yet only a year before this, during the winter 1825-26 when there had been a financial panic, he had displayed at length one of his genuine old Tory prejudices and had advertised his contempt for "every variety of that arch class of quacks, who call themselves political economists". He had done this by writing his *Paper Money Lyrics,* the satire of which is based, of course, on that ubiquitous crotchet of his, the mistrust of bank notes. In these verses, Peacock combines both political and literary satire, for the subject throughout is the financial situation, but in the individual verses a number of contemporary poets, Southey, Wordsworth, Coleridge, Moore, Scott and Campbell, are somewhat crudely parodied, usually by the imitation of particular poems. The Scots, because of their pound notes and their economists and Peacock's prejudice against the whole nation, are throughout conspicuous. Topical in interest and purely superficial as literary parodies, the *Paper Money Lyrics* are of no importance now, though it is not difficult to understand their success at the time, when they were handed round to Peacock's friends in manuscript. They were not printed, it is said, out of respect for James Mill, now Peacock's superior at the India Office. It was not until 1837 that several of them were published in a periodical called the *Guide*, edited by Peacock's friend, Henry Cole; and then the whole collection was brought out privately in an edition of a hundred copies.

There were no more articles and reviews from Peacock until 1830, when the *Westminster* once again handed over the unfortunate Moore to him. The book was the first volume of Moore's *Letters and Journals of Lord Byron*. It was in planning his offensive against this volume that Peacock made a very good friend, for he enlisted the aid of Hobhouse, who would not openly assist the reviewer but nevertheless laid with him the foundations of a lifelong friendship. Unfortunately, Peacock's undue severity in this notice brought about a quarrel between Moore and Bowring, the editor of the *Westminster*, so that the second volume was neither offered nor accepted for review, which is our loss because Peacock intended to examine the character of Byron at length in his notice of the second volume of the *Letters and Journals.* From a few scattered references and the Mr. Cypress passages in *Nightmare Abbey,* we can form a dim idea of Peacock's estimate of Byron's character, of which his examination would have been unfavourable, a trifle unjust, but very shrewd. It would be hard to indicate the weakness of Byronism more briefly and pointedly than it is indicated in the following remark of Mr. Hilary to Mr. Cypress: "You talk like a Rosicrucian, who will love nothing but a sylph, who does not believe in the existence of a sylph, and who yet quarrels with the whole universe for not containing a sylph."

The *Westminster* had two more reviews from him during the same year. One was a notice of *The Memoirs, Correspondence, and Private Papers of Thomas Jefferson,* in which Peacock's leaning towards a stately and philosophical and very eighteenth-century Republicanism is clearly shown. The other contribution, noticing some Parliamentary Reports on London Bridge and some *Chronicles of London Bridge: By an Antiquary,* is a defence of the then existing bridge and a spirited attack upon the proposal for building a new one, which Peacock objects to not on the grounds of sentiment (though, in reality, his dislike of innovation was probably at the root of the matter and encouraged him to find reasons) but on those of utility. The removal of the old dam would flood the city, he points out, and proceeds to paint a very Peacockian picture of a London half submerged. More Peacockian still, however, are his remarks on the old bridge:

The old London Bridge was begun in 1176, and finished in 1209. It was built on such unscientific principles, that it ought to have been carried away before it was finished, when it was finished, and at any given time subsequently; but partly by the awkward contrivance of barbarous men, partly by its own obstinacy, it has stood six centuries and a quarter, amidst the perpetual prophecies of disinterested engineers that it could not stand any longer: while one bridge after another, on different parts of the same river, in which no son of science had espied a flaw, has wilfully tumbled to pieces, by the sinking of the piers, or the yielding of the abutments, in despite of the most mathematical demonstrations of the absurdity of such a proceeding.

There is no mistaking these accents.

The voice is that of Peacock in his very prime. This is his most productive and successful period. The year before 1830 had seen the publication of his *Misfortunes of Elphin,* and the year after brought *Crotchet Castle* into the world. Thus the best two books he ever wrote had less than a full two years between their dates of publication, a fact of some interest and significance when we consider the very irregular progress of his work. There are seven years between *Maid Marian* and *The Misfortunes of Elphin,* and there are no less than thirty between *Crotchet Castle* and its successor, *Gryll Grange.* It is not difficult to see why this particular period of his life should have been so fruitful. He had arrived at maturity; he was happy in his marriage and had settled down to his work at India House, and neither his home nor his office were as yet making very great demands on his time and attention. A little later the situation was changed. His wife gradually grew worse, and the great age and subsequent death of his mother (who had done what she could to manage affairs at home for him) left him with a growing family and an ailing wife on his hands. His work as an official did not remain an easy routine, and though it may never have been arduous, it soon became more engrossing as more and more responsible duties were added to it. This explains in part that long silence which followed *Crotchet Castle*. Any further explanation is supplied by the scope and temper of Peacock's mind. He was not naturally prolific or inventive, and as he was not in want of money nor particularly desirous of applause he lacked the stimulus that has made so many authors write books when they have had nothing to say. As a man of letters, Peacock was essentially an amateur, a fact worth remembering because it explains a good many of his characteristics both as novelist and critic, and even as a poet. He wrote primarily for his own good pleasure.

This was perhaps as well, for the first of his two little masterpieces, *The Misfortunes of Elphin,* attracted little notice when it was first published—it was not reprinted for nearly fifty years—and has never had its due since except from a little handful of critics. It is one of the shortest of his tales, but we may hazard the guess that in both the initial preparation and the actual writing it gave him the most trouble of them all. In this story of legendary Welsh heroes, Peacock retains and develops the method he had employed in *Maid Marian,* the treatment of romantic material satirically. In *The Misfortunes of Elphin* the material is even more wildly romantic, and the treatment is even more closely sardonic. Even the idyllic background, ever present in the earlier story, has largely disappeared, and only a few fine descriptive passages, in which his enthusiasm for the Welsh mountain scenery plays its part, are left for romance. All the rest is humour, now far less violently farcical, and irony, and this last is the very atmosphere in which the little tale has its being.

Peacock planned this story far more carefully than he had done *Maid Marian,* and Sir Edward Strachey has told us how he had heard Peacock "say that he had great difficulty in getting at the true story of Taliesin's birth, as more than one learned authority had concealed his own ignorance on the matter by saying that the story was too long to be told then". He had picked up a little Welsh during his early visits to the country, and as his wife is said to have been familiar with both the language and its old literature, no doubt she was able to assist him. His chief authorities seem to have been *The Myvyrian Archaiology,* a collection of ancient Welsh poems, many of which he paraphrased and introduced into his narrative (though the best poem there is his own, *The War Song of Dinas Vawr*) ; and *The Cambro-Briton,* whose English translations of the old Welsh triads he frequently quotes. The basis of his story is the legendary material grouped about the figure of Taliesin, the greatest of the bards, though Peacock only makes use of part of this material, eliminates the more supernatural events, and introduces a love affair between Taliesin and Elphin's daughter, Melanghel, that is not found in the original. He also pressed into service two other legends, the inundation of the Great Plain of Gwaelod owing to the carelessness of Seithenyn, and the kidnapping of Queen Gwenyvar by King Melvas. These respectively provide him with the events of the opening and the closing chapters. The introduction of the Seithenyn legend was a particularly happy stroke, for out of it Peacock contrives the richest

and most picturesque scenes in the tale, and its greatest
character, the best of all his comic figures. Seithenyn
himself. Parts of this gentleman's glorious speech, in
which he protests against the embankment being touched
although it is rotten, are a very clever parody of some
of Canning's speeches against Parliamentary reform, but
Seithenyn himself is not Mr. Anyside Antijack over
again, is not, indeed, a caricature of Canning in any
sense, but is a genuine individual creation, one of literature's immortal topers.

Crotchet Castle, the only other novel of Peacock's
worthy of a place by the side of *The Misfortunes of
Elphin,* followed it fairly closely, being written during
1830, and published early in the new year. It attracted
more attention from the reviews than its predecessors had
done, and very quickly established itself as a favourite
with Peacock's admirers. It was also chosen as the
object of one of those indiscriminate slatings that so
disfigure the periodical criticism of that time, and, curiously enough, this angry notice appeared in the very
magazine, *Fraser's,* to which Peacock afterwards contributed a number of essays and the only other novel
he ever wrote. Like so many of those famous slashing
reviews, this notice is so roundly and wildly abusive
that it is completely wide of the mark. The critic is
so furious that he will not take time and trouble to
be discriminating. Thus, he tells his readers that
Peacock is an "ignorant, stupid, poor devil, who has
no fun, little learning, no facility, no *easiness*". Now,
it would not be difficult for a determined adverse critic
to make capital out of Peacock's obvious limitations as
a novelist, but this reviewer, in his blind wrath, has
merely tried to attack Peacock where he is absolutely

impregnable. Whatever Peacock may have been, he was obviously neither ignorant nor stupid, and it is precisely fun, learning, facility and easiness that are plainly discovered in *Crotchet Castle*. It is an unconquerable fortress of wit and scholarship.

Abandoning the satirical romance, Peacock returns in this novel to his earlier manner. *Crotchet Castle,* like *Headlong Hall, Melincourt,* and *Nightmare Abbey,* may be described as a novel of opinion. It has more in common with *Headlong Hall,* however, than it has with the other two. In them Peacock takes a definite standpoint, satirising reactionary sentiment and opinion in *Melincourt* and ultra-romantic tendencies in *Nightmare Abbey.* In *Crochet Castle,* as in *Headlong Hall,* the satire is general and the author's own standpoint cannot be discovered, but the passage of fifteen years has brought the writer even nearer to a universal scepticism, so that the satire in this later and riper book is always merging into absolute humour. The scheme is the old familiar one, the gathering of a number of crotcheteers at a country house owned by a gentleman whose chief duty is to keep the bottle in brisk circulation. There is, however, more movement than in *Headlong Hall,* for the whole party makes a voyage up the Thames and finally lands in Wales, and two love stories, that of Captain Fitzchrome and Lady Clorinda and that of Mr. Chainmail and Susannah Touchandgo, give the novel some semblance of a plot. There is an unusually large number of characters in *Crotchet Castle,* but only a very few of them are caricatures of actual individuals. Poor Coleridge once more appears, this time as Mr. Skionar, but is treated far more sympathetically than he was before. His "two dear friends, Mr. Wilful Wontsee and Mr. Rumblesack Shantsee" are, of course, Wordsworth and Southey. These are all that are left of the old gang. Mr. MacQuedy (that is, Mac—Q.E.D., the son of a demonstration—a typical example of Peacock's method of nomenclature) is J. R. MacCulloch, professor of Political Economy in the then recently founded London University and a friend of the Mills. Mr. Toogood was probably intended for Robert Owen. The other minor characters are simply crotcheteers, each representing some dominating interest: Mr. Philpot cares for nothing but rivers, Mr. Trillo for nothing but opera, Mr. Henbane for nothing but poisons; Mr. Firedamp is terrified of water; Mr. Eavesdrop is a familiar type of journalist who was then just beginning his career of turning other people's hospitality to good uses; and so on and so forth. Standing above these are certain characters who are more roundly drawn. Mr. Chainmail believes that life was at its best in the twelfth century and so is one of the crotcheteers, but is presented as a pleasant and manly youth. Miss Touchandgo is the typical romantic young girl. The worldly-wise Lady Clorinda, who after so many little cynicisms marries her poor young man in the end, is the best of all Peacock's women characters, being something more than a mere figure-head. She might be described as a nineteenth-century Millamant. Towering above them all is the Reverend Doctor Folliott, the avowed enemy of all cant, rebellion, talk of progress and the like, and the friend of learning and good living, equally adept at laying out a debater with his wit or a footpad with his cudgel. Peacock undoubtedly put a good deal of himself into this highly successful character, but he is a genuine creation and not a mere mouthpiece, so that it is a mistake to assume, as so many critics have assumed, that the Doctor's opinions are necessarily the author's.

It is this mistake of identifying the author with his chief character that has led so many critics to exaggerate the conservative trend of Peacock's mind at the time when he wrote *Crotchet Castle*. He was growing more and more conservative about some things (and Dr. Folliott and, in a lesser degree, Mr. Chainmail are there in the book to express this side of his mind), but he was still something of a Radical too. He is such a curious mixture that he cannot easily be claimed by one party or the other, and this is particularly true of him in *Crotchet Castle,* in which he is really far more detached than he had been in any other novel of opinion. It happened, however, that one prominent personage had contrived to offend both the Tory and the Radical sides of his mind, and upon him Peacock fell with fury. This was Brougham, who never appears in the novel but is nevertheless the chief victim of its satire. The "learned friend", as Dr. Folliott always calls him, was the pillar of the Society for the Diffusion of Popular Knowledge, which represented everything that was objectionable to the Tory scholar in Peacock, who disliked, too, the officious busy-bodying that found its way into many of Brougham's activities, such as the setting up of Charity Commissioners and the like. On the other hand, Brougham's gradual defection from the Liberal cause, which resulted in his taking office as Lord Chancellor at the very time when *Crotchet Castle* was being written, offended the Radical in Peacock. And behind all this, giving an undue severity to the satire, is an obvious dislike of the man himself. Brougham, with his restless vanity, his officiousness, his love of the lime-light, was the type of man that Peacock could not help detesting. In their virtues and vices, the two men were poles apart. For the rest, *Crotchet Castle* is best described as a satire upon contemporary cant of every description, and a humorous exploitation, the most thorough that Peacock ever gave us, of the crotchet, the dispropor-tionate emphasis upon one opinion or interest. As such it is the richest and ripest of all his novels.

During the next few years Peacock wrote extremely little. He attended the opera and ballet fairly regularly, and wrote notices for the *Globe and Traveller* and *The Examiner*. To the short-lived *London Review,* which the Philosophical Radicals founded in 1835, he con-tributed four articles, two on musical subjects, and the other two, "French Comic Romances" and "The Epicier", on literature. Later in the 'thirties, several short pieces, prose and verse, found their way into *The Guide* and *Bentley's Miscellany*. But his most important piece of writing during this period was neither in the form of a review nor a few satirical or sentimental verses, but was a certain "Memorandum respecting the Application of Steam Navigation to the internal and external Com-munications of India", which formidable document takes us back to that India House where we had left him early in the present chapter. He was appointed, after two years' probation, one of four assistants to the Examiner, his duty being to attend to the despatches of the Department of Public Works. In 1823 one of the four, James Mill, was promoted to Assistant-Examiner, and Peacock's salary was raised to £1000. Seven years later Mill became Examiner and his former position was left unfilled, while Strachey and Peacock were called Senior Assistants and given £1200 each, probably sharing the work of Mill's former department, that of Revenue, between them. In 1836 Strachey died and Peacock then became Assistant-Examiner, but before the summer was out, Mill also died, and Peacock became Examiner at a salary of £2000, remaining in office at that salary for the next twenty years. Thus he became one of the chief officials of the largest trading company the world has ever known, whose revenue was greater than that of many European kingdoms.

We know very little about Peacock's life as an official. Most of his work was necessarily confidential, and he was not the type of man who discusses his affairs at length with his friends. He held himself aloof from his subordinates, and he corresponded as infrequently as possible with his few friends, so that there is little or nothing to be gleaned from his letters. We do know, however, that he was an extremely capable official. On several occasions he acted as the Company's representative. Thus, in 1834, when J. S. Buckingham, a former M.P. for Sheffield, brought an action against the Company because he had been expelled from India, and in 1836, when the Liverpool merchants tried to break the Company's salt monopoly, Peacock was the advocate for India House, and on each occasion showed considerable skill, making full use of his undoubted ability to accumulate evidence and to state a case coolly and clearly. His other public appearances were all connected with a twofold problem that he had made his own, the problem of speeding up communication with India. Here Peacock not only performed a notable service for his Company but also for his country, becoming a public benefactor. Hundreds of men who had never set eyes on *Nightmare Abbey* or *Crotchet Castle* knew and honoured the name of Thomas Love Peacock because it was largely owing to his foresight and tenacity that communication with India was immeasurably improved. Readers of *Stalky and Co.* will remember how Beetle, browsing in the Headmaster's library, found there some "little tales of a heady and bewildering nature, interspersed with unusual songs— Peacock was that writer's name". Beetle and his friends should have been told that if it had not been for the activities of "that writer", their grandfathers, when they were young men grilling in the Plains, would not have had such frequent letters from home.

Not long after Peacock joined the Company, there was a good deal of dissatisfaction, particularly among the merchants in India, with the system of communications. Mails were still carried by sail round the Cape of Good Hope, and only arrived at India House twice a year. In 1829 the Directors of the Company, who had been slow to move in the matter but had at last given permission for a trial voyage in the Red Sea, handed the problem over to Peacock. It was a twofold problem because there was the question of using steam power instead of sail and there was the further question of shortening the route. This could be done either by going through Egypt and thence by the Red Sea or by crossing Syria and travelling down the Euphrates into the Persian Gulf. Peacock considered the question of these alternative routes and made a number of queries, which were forwarded to Capt. Chesney, then on a mission in Egypt. We have Chesney's evidence that these queries were unusually valuable, and that when he returned to England in 1832 and met Peacock at the India Office, he "found that he was deeply versed in the ancient history of the Euphrates, and that he had not only been the first to bring this line of communication with India forward, but that he had collected in a thick book every private notice he could find of that river, whether contained in Gibbon, Balbi, or any other work". Evidently Peacock's methodical scholarly habit was already bearing fruit. Later the question was referred to a Parliamentary Select Committee, and Peacock was called upon to give his testimony. He favoured the Euphrates route, particularly for mails, and pointed out the necessity of forestalling Russia. The Government finally sent out an expedition to the Euphrates under the command of Chesney.

In 1837 another Select Committee met to consider the question of steam navigation, and Peacock, representing the Company, was the principal witness. He discussed the various problems at great length, and contrived to make one or two very Peacockian remarks, such as "I am not aware that it would be any benefit to the people of India to send Europeans amongst them". From now onwards Peacock worked hard to secure for the Company a fleet of iron steamers, and by 1839 six were in commission. Two of these, the *Pluto* and *Proserpine,* were built in London, and he was able to supervise both their construction and the various test voyages they made before they were finally sent round the Cape. Five of these vessels were used during the Chinese campaign. Thus Peacock became something of an authority on steam navigation, and was proud of his "iron chickens", as he called the ships that had been brought into existence largely through his efforts. But not only did this work absorb a great deal of his time and energy, but the improved communication it brought about added to his duties. In the old days, when there were only two Indian mails a year, the officials in the Examiner's Office, who attended to the various despatches, had little or nothing to do for long periods. Peacock's well-known verse on an India House day refers to those leisurely times:

> From ten to eleven, ate a breakfast for seven:
> From eleven to noon, to begin 'twas too soon;
> From twelve to one, asked "What's to be done?"
> From one to two, found nothing to do;
> From two to three, began to foresee
> That from three to four would be a damned bore.

Those officials who arrived by ten were provided with breakfast by this extraordinarily paternal Company, and by four, of course, all was over. Incidentally, it is said that Lamb, whose work was not in the Examiner's department and who never had any such difficulty in getting through the day, resented these lines, which must not, however, be taken too seriously as a description of Peacock's early duties. But by the time Peacock had become Examiner and his steamers were afloat, the Indian mail arrived every month, so that the Examiner's Office could never be idle long. There is little more to be said about Peacock as an official. We know that he was punctual and methodical and industrious, and one of his subordinates, P. A. Daniel, records that he was always kind to his juniors but always remained aloof, unlike John Stuart Mill, who frequently left his office to have a chat with the clerks outside. Peacock, always self-contained, grew more and more reserved as the years went by, and divided his time between Lower Halliford and Leadenhall Street, India and Ancient Athens.

"And a precious good place he has too," Thackeray made his little clerk exclaim, at the thought of Peacock. That Peacock had a precious good place there can be no doubt: he had one of the most comfortable posts in a very comfortable age. Though his duties and responsibilities multiplied with the years, it would be idle to pretend that even during his busiest period he had not leisure enough to write if he wanted to write. Most of his evenings and his week-ends were free, and if he did not write it was largely because there was nothing he wanted to say that was urgent or amusing enough to take him from his books. Had he not been so comfortably situated, with a pleasant routine of work at one end of his daily journey and a pleasant old library waiting for him at the other end, he might have written more, either for money or to amuse himself, but it is doubtful if he would have written anything of great value. Like most men, he contrived to say all that he really had to say before he had done. That a humorist and minor poet should have been so successful not as a mere clerk but as a responsible high official may seem very strange at first sight, but there is nothing strange about the matter to any one who is solidly acquainted with Peacock's novels, fantastic as they may seem. His first entrance into the Company's service was undoubtedly a stroke of fortune; but substantial merit and not luck explains the rest of his history there. An examination of a few pages of his prose shows us why he was as likely to be as able an official as either of the two Mills, the economist who preceded him or the philosopher who followed him. He had a clear, realistic, tenacious mind, with a firm grasp of fact and a gift for lucid exposition. He had the humorist's fine sense of proportion, without which the ridiculous is never observed. He had the satirist's logical habit of mind, which so frequently displays the streak of absurdity in opinions by taking them to their logical conclusion. He had the methodical solitary student's ability to master a new subject swiftly and surely. All the references to him as an official testify to the presence in his daily work of these qualities and habits of mind, and thus we have no reason to be surprised that he should have been so successful in a double capacity, finding not only a comfortable livelihood but even honours where so few men of letters have found them.

CHAPTER IV

LATER LIFE AND CHARACTER

PEACOCK continued for some time living in rooms in London during the week and only spending his week-ends with his family at Lower Halliford. But when the railways made a daily journey possible, from Walton station close by, he left London altogether, merely travelling up to the office and then hurrying back to his library and garden by the Thames as soon as the day's work was done. His wife's long illness and his own indifference to society combined to make him almost a recluse. During the last thirty years of his life his closest friend was John Cam Hobhouse, Lord Broughton, and when he left home during the later 'thirties and the 'forties, it was usually to stay with Broughton at Erle Stoke, Westbury, where he was a great favourite with all the family. Thackeray mentions him in a letter he wrote, in 1850, to Mrs. Brook-field, and the country house at which they were both guests was probably Erle Stoke. "Peacock", Thackeray writes, naming the guests "—did you ever read *Headlong Hall* and *Maid Marian?*—a charming lyrical poet and Horatian satirist, he was when a writer; now he is a white-headed jolly old worldling, full of information about India and everything else in the world".

Thackeray little imagined, when he spoke of Peacock as a writer in the past tense, that still another novel by the author of *Headlong Hall* was to appear, after another eleven years. It may have been at Broughton's table that Macaulay met Peacock on the very last day of 1851, under which date Macaulay writes in his journal:

I met Peacock; a very clever fellow, and a good scholar. I am glad to have an opportunity of being better acquainted with him. We had out Aristophanes, Æschylus, Sophocles, and several other old fellows, and tried each other's quality pretty well. We are both strong enough in these matters for gentlemen.

But for Peacock such visits and encounters were rare events.

His own domestic life, however, was by no means uneventful. In January 1844 his eldest daughter, Mary Ellen, married a young naval officer, Edward Nicolls, and within three months was widowed by his death at sea. Four years later, Mrs. Nicolls was living in London with her brother, Edward Gryffydh Peacock, and they were both members of a little set of literary aspirants. This set included one Richard Stephen Charnock, a solicitor, and very soon it also included Charnock's young articled clerk, a poor, clever, very ambitious youth who had been educated in Germany. This was George Meredith. In 1848 a manuscript magazine called *The Monthly Observer* was brought out, and Meredith, young Peacock, and Mrs. Nicolls, all contributors, became great friends. Mrs. Nicolls had beauty and wit and very soon Meredith found himself in love with her. She was nine years older than he was and had a daughter of five; he had neither means nor prospects;

nevertheless, he proposed marriage, five times it is said, without success. Finally the brilliant, handsome and impetuous youth swept away her doubts and scruples, and in August 1849 they were married. They went abroad for a short time, returned to live in seaside lodgings, and then settled down at Weybridge. While there, in 1851, Meredith published his first volume of poems, which was dedicated to "Thomas Love Peacock, Esq., with the profound admiration and affectionate respect of his son-in-law". Two years later, the Merediths, who had not prospered, went to live with Peacock, who was now a widower, his wife having died in 1851. Their son, Arthur Gryffydh, was born under his grandfather's roof in June 1853. Peacock, however, soon found a baby, an exuberant and restless son-in-law, a young couple given to hot disputes, too much for him, and so he quickly installed them in a small house across the green, Vine Cottage, where Meredith wrote his *Shaving of Shagpat*. There is no need to record in detail the history of this ill-fated marriage. It is sufficient to say that Meredith and his wife could not agree, and that after frequent scenes and separations, Mrs. Meredith left the country in 1858 with Henry Wallis, the artist, returned during the following year, a sick and wretched woman, deprived of her son and unforgiven by her husband, and died in 1861.

This association with Meredith is undoubtedly the most interesting passage in Peacock's later life. Unfortunately we know very little about it. The breach between Meredith and his wife cut him off from Peacock, and the tragic conclusion not unnaturally sealed the lips of both men. Meredith rarely men-

tioned his association with Peacock, whose very name
would only recall a host of painful memories. That
Peacock should have said little does not greatly matter.
We gather that he was not overfond of his son-in-law,
whose German education, lack of interest in formal
scholarship, and markedly different temperament and
outlook, would not find favour in the eyes of a man
forty-three years his senior, who detested all things
German, loved formal scholarship, and had no particular fondness for brilliant, restless young men. On
the other hand, there can be no doubt that Meredith
himself, who had a genuine admiration for Peacock's
work, was considerably influenced by the older man,
whose seniority and prestige and very sharply defined
attitude towards life and literature made him a companion whose influence would have to be actively and
consciously resisted if it were not to take effect. Nor
must it be forgotten that during the time the two men
were in close touch with one another, Meredith was
very young, very impressionable, and as yet uncertain
as to the kind of work he would do. It is of course
a commonplace of criticism that there are traces of
Peacock himself in some of Meredith's characters,
notably Dr. Middleton. But their association had far
more important results for Meredith's work than such
hints for characterisation. What Peacock probably did
was to influence Meredith in shaping the whole course
of his future work. When they first met Meredith
was a vaguely romantic poet. Shortly after they parted
he became the creator of a new kind of fiction, in which
romantic narrative is fused with intellectual comedy.
What was it that turned his attention to Comedy, which
he created in his best novels and criticised so admirably

in his *Essay?* Undoubtedly it was in part the influence of that close and enthusiastic student of Comedy, that indefatigable servant of the Comic Spirit, Thomas Love Peacock.

The December number of *Fraser's Magazine* in 1851 contained a long article entitled "Gastronomy and Civilization", in which there is some sturdy praise of food and drink, much curious gastronomical scholarship, and an account of the art of dining in various stages of civilisation and under various forms of government. The article is signed "M. M." and the writer is Mary Meredith, Peacock's eldest daughter. There is good evidence, apart from the article itself, that Peacock himself had a hand in its composition, and it was probably he who suggested both the subject and the method of its treatment. Some parts of it were probably written by him. Such passages as this—". . . it is still a question whether they would not have exercised a more beneficial influence, and have been better men, if they had moistened their throats with Madeira, and enlarged their sympathies with grouse"—are pure Peacock. During the following year, he openly appeared as a contributor to the same magazine with a series of leisurely articles on classical drama called *Horae Dramaticae,* articles full of valuable scholarship and critical good sense. The first was on the Latin comedy, *Querolus; or, the Buried Treasure,* and appeared in the March number. The second was on *The Phaëton of Euripides,* and appeared in the next number. But the third, and the last of the series, did not emerge until the autumn of 1857, when Peacock made his subject, "The Flask of Cratinus", a peg on which to hang a very characteristic dissertation on poetry and good liquor, together with some observations on the mixing of wine and water. He had now retired from the India House and was able to devote his mornings to leisurely composition. Two more articles found their way into *Fraser's* in 1858, "Chapelle and Bachaumont", which has some admirable translations in it, and "Demetrius Galanus". In addition, he contributed a long review of Müller and Donaldson's *History of Greek Literature* to the magazine, and, as a contrast to all these articles, his moving little verses, already mentioned in connection with his early love affair, *Newark Abbey*.

The remaining two compositions that found their way into *Fraser's* are of much greater importance. The first is the famous *Memoirs of Shelley*, made up of four separate contributions: an article that appeared in the July number of 1858, reviewing Hogg's *Life of Shelley,* Trelawney's *Recollections of the Last Days of Shelley and Byron,* and another volume on Shelley by one Middleton; a further article, contributed to the January number of 1860, reviewing the *Shelley Memorials;* a collection of Shelley's letters from Italy, with a short introductory note, which appeared in the March number of 1860; and, finally, a Supplementary Notice, contributed two years later, written in reply to an article by Richard Garnett, who had attacked Peacock, and to another article that had appeared in the *Quarterly*. All these were reprinted in the three volume edition of Peacock's works edited by Sir Henry Cole, and have since been published separately, in a volume edited by Mr. Brett-Smith for the Oxford University Press. They have a very important place among Shelley documents. Having been in close touch with Shelley, as we have already seen, during the period

that covers the separation from Harriet, the elopement
and subsequent return, and Harriet's death, Peacock was
more favourably placed than any of Shelley's biographers.
He himself had no intention of writing a biography,
and in the introductory paragraphs of his *Memoirs* he
gives reasons why he had already refused to undertake
such a task:

No man is bound to write the life of another. No
man who does so is bound to tell the public all he knows.
On the contrary, he is bound to keep to himself whatever
may injure the interests or hurt the feelings of the living,
especially when the latter have in no way injured or calum-
niated the dead, and are not necessarily brought before the
tribunal of public opinion in the character of either plaintiffs
or defendants.

The whole subject of Shelley's private life, he considered, were best left alone.

I could have wished that, like Wordsworth's Cuckoo,
he had been allowed to remain a voice and a mystery:
that, like his own Skylark, he had been left unseen in his
congenial region,

> Above the smoke and stir of this dim spot
> Which men call earth,

and that he had been only heard in the splendour of his
song.

In this instance, many of us, who do not necessarily
see eye to eye with Peacock on the subject of biography,
will find ourselves in wistful agreement with him. All
too frequently the light that comes flashing with
Shelley's name has shown us nothing but a body of
wrangling biographers. The name of his unfortunate
first wife has almost become a synonym for that
retrospective scandal-mongering which passes in some

quarters for an enthusiasm for literature. And the poet himself has suffered, perhaps more than any other poet has ever suffered, from the furious partisanship of his more unbalanced admirers, who have used his very weaknesses as a stick to beat the whole age in which he lived, and from the inevitable reaction of critics, hitherto impartial, who have simply been goaded into attack.

Peacock then explains why he should be writing about Shelley :

But since it is not to be so, since so much has been, and so much more will probably be, written about him, the motives which deterred me from originating a substantive work on the subject, do not restrict me from commenting on what has been published by others, and from correcting errors, if such should appear to me to occur, in the narratives which I may pass under review.

Thus his aim in bringing to light his own memories of the poet is to correct what seem to him errors of fact or wrong impressions in the existing biographies. Having once set to work, he does a great deal more than that, indeed provides us with one of the most valuable and amusing accounts of Shelley we possess, undoubtedly the most balanced, veracious and acute record written by any of Shelley's actual companions. It is true that it is written with a certain air of detachment and reserve, but nobody who knew Peacock could suppose that he could tell the story in any other way. Nor must the relish with which he exhibits the comic side of his friend be mistaken for common malice, for Peacock, not being a perfervid and humourless hero-worshipper, saw no reason why his friend should not be comic, and, once more, it must not be forgotten that while his readers only saw

Shelley as a poetic genius who died young, Peacock also saw a youth several years his junior and his companion in many an odd scrape. In talk Peacock would never tolerate the least abuse of Shelley, though—as we learn from Robert Buchanan's account of his visits to Peacock—he admitted in talk certain facts, such as Shelley's passionate and violent temper, that never found their way into his printed record. The two points on which he was insistent, correcting one or other of the biographers, were the fact that Shelley and Harriet were not separated by mutual consent and the fact that Shelley constantly suffered from hallucinations. Great efforts have been made to prove that he was wrong on both these counts but, except in certain small details, such efforts have failed. His belief that there was no estrangement between Shelley and Harriet before Mary Godwin arrived on the scene is now no longer generally accepted, though there is every excuse for his holding such a belief if only because it is quite possible that Shelley deliberately refrained from taking Peacock into his full confidence on the subject of his relations with Harriet. Peacock was Harriet's friend and had, too, an uncomfortable habit of giving short shrift to Shelley's illusions, and there can be no doubt that Shelley was nursing one or two concerning his wife at that time. For the rest, Peacock was in the right and his attitude throughout towards both Harriet and Shelley is in pleasant contrast to that of so many persons who have fished in these dangerous waters. And though it is possible that he was wrong about one of Shelley's famous adventures, the reality of which he flatly denied, his account of the poet's various hallucinations and his discussion of them, brief though it is, threw a stronger light on his subject's character than it had known before and made possible further and closer studies. Peacock was fortunately placed in being an eye-witness who was also the possessor of a critical mind, and, for all his reserve and reluctance, his testimony is supremely valuable, perhaps unique. As one of his editors, Mr. Brett-Smith, has justly observed: "The great value of the *Memoirs* lies in their standpoint: they attain the just blend of sympathy and discernment which the nature of their subject makes so difficult".

The other contribution to *Fraser's* was nothing less than a full-length novel, indeed, the longest of all his novels except *Melincourt*. This was *Gryll Grange,* which appeared as a serial in *Fraser's* in 1860 and was published in volume form early in the following year. Peacock was seventy-five when he turned again to fiction, after a lapse of thirty years. But *Gryll Grange* was not his first attempt to return to fiction, as a number of fragments amply testify. In three of these, *Chertsey, Cotswold Chace* and *St. Katherine,* it was evidently his intention to make use of his early memories, to which, as we know, he returned in this ripe old age of his, but his powers of invention, never very strong, apparently failed him every time, after he made several promising and characteristic openings. So he fell back, in *Gryll Grange,* on the old easy plan. Squire Gryll lives comfortably with his pretty niece, on the borders of the New Forest. The local clergyman, Dr. Opimian, is his good friend and frequent table-companion. In the Forest is a cultivated though rather eccentric young man named Falconer, who is discovered, living in a

remote tower and served by seven charming maidens,
by Dr. Opimian and introduced into the Gryll circle.
There are other visitors to the Grange, notably Mr.
MacBorrowdale, who is both a Scot and an economist
but is not unsympathetically presented, and Lord
Curryfin, who lectures on fish and is apparently brought
in as a butt, but who, nevertheless, contrives to escape
his creator's mockery long before the end of the story
is reached.   There are several love affairs, pleasantly
sketched in, but the greater part of the novel circles
about the composition and production of a satirical
comedy on the Greek model, *Aristophanes in London*.
This entertaining little comedy in verse describes how
Gryllus is awakened from his three thousand years'
sleep by Circe and is summoned by three spirit-rappers
to London, where he has once more to decide whether
it is better to be a beast than a man. He is allowed to
question a number of reformers, scientific, moral, edu-
cational, political, and comes to the conclusion that
the world is worse than it was before. He is then
confronted with seven competitive examiners, who are
seen later rejecting a number of military candidates
from the shades, among them Hannibal and Oliver
Cromwell and Richard Cœur-de-Lion. All further
attempts to make Gryllus "feel conviction of our
superior greatness" completely fail, but he is willing
to stay for supper, and the comedy ends with the
chorus :

> Shadows to-night have offered portraits true
> Of many follies which the world entrall.
> "Shadows we are, and shadows we pursue";
> But, in the banquet's well-illumined hall,
> Realities, delectable to all,
> Invite you now our festal joy to share.

This little comedy provides us with a key to the spirit of the whole novel. Almost every tendency of the age is pilloried in these chapters. In one respect, this is probably the most interesting of Peacock's novels to the average modern reader because the world he satirises in it is essentially the modern world. All that has happened since is that most of these molehills that Peacock turns into mountains have now actually become mountains. Pretentious scientists, spirit-rapping, newspapers, the craze for speed, bad food, competitive examinations, the United States and all their works, social science, cheap mechanical education, commercialism—these are some of Peacock's chief targets, and not only are these things still with us but now they almost hide the sky. The world of to-day might be described as Dr. Opimian's nightmare. But though Peacock makes a few cuts at Lord Facing-both-ways (Brougham) and Lord Michin Malicho (Lord John Russell), there is very little personal satire in *Gryll Grange*. Its characters are brought on to talk agreeably and though the majority can hardly be considered human beings, at least they are not personified opinions. The old hard hitting has vanished with the old high spirits. Dr. Opimian may be Dr. Folliott over again, but he is a far gentler and less caustic commentator on the follies of this world. *Gryll Grange* may reveal Peacock as an old man, surveying a world he does not like, but there is here no trace of that bitterness and despair which so often find their way into the reactionary records of old age. In their place is a ripe geniality, a smile and shrug of the mind. Even Brougham himself, we feel, would be given his seat at the board and his part in the easy, learned talk if he should make his appearance at *Gryll*

Grange. "On the whole," we find Dr. Opimian remarking, "I agree in opinion with Theseus, that there is more good than evil in the world." His wife tells him that he would not maintain any opinion if he had not an authority two thousand years old for it. He replies: "Well, my dear, I think most opinions worth maintaining have an authority of about that age."

Gryll Grange is full of opinions that are at least two thousand years old. It will have nothing to do with any complacent cant about progress, but nevertheless it contrives to find more good than evil in the world. Indeed, though we have noticed its satire first, we do not think of it as a piece of satire. It is significant, too, that although it has as much action in it as the earlier novels, perhaps more than some, we hardly remember it as having any at all. It remains in the memory as a volume of quaint table-talk. The characters seat themselves at the board or go walking in the garden or the Forest, remote from the smoke and bustle and babble of the world, and discuss and illustrate and cap quotations. The Vestal Virgins and their hair, the complexion of Cleopatra, Greek drawing and perspective, the game of quadrille, the bald Venus of the Romans, Athenian comedy, ghosts in literature, these and other topics, illustrated by not a little out-of-the-way scholarship and innumerable quotations from Greek, Latin, English, Italian, French authors, for the most part from those who were Peacock's favourites, pass the easy and convivial hours. Now and then one of the ladies will sing a song, and the best of these songs is one of Peacock's most delightful poems, *Love and Age*. But there are no more rousing drinking choruses just as

there are no more hot disputations. We have returned
from Illyria to Arden, where "they fleet the time
carelessly as they did in the golden world". The
garden, the Forest, the table bright with candles;
and somewhere a daft roaring world filled with
reformers and canters and ranters; some books, a
little music, young people falling in and out of love,
the bottle happily circulating while the shining ball
of talk is flung across the table: such is *Gryll
Grange*. It would be idle to pretend that it is one
of Peacock's best performances. There is here only
a genial echo of that old ironic voice, and the Peacockian essence, so richly distilled in *The Misfortunes
of Elphin* and *Crotchet Castle,* is here so watered
down that the palate only recognises a ghost of the
old flavour. Yet not only was its mere composition something of a feat, but there is probably no admirer of its
author who does not delight in it, perhaps regard it with
a special affection. With its suggestion of sunset and
mellow age, of old themes retouched with geniality, it is
perhaps an ideal *envoi*.

The tastes of Dr. Opimian, we are told, were four:
a good library, a good dinner, a pleasant garden, and
rural walks. These, too, were Peacock's tastes, and
he passed his retirement at Lower Halliford enjoying
them. He rose early as a rule, and spent all day
either in his library or his garden. Visitors were few,
not being encouraged. His granddaughter gives us
a charming little sketch of him as he was during these
years:

In society my grandfather was ever a welcome guest,
his genial manner, hearty appreciation of wit and humour
in others, and the amusing way in which he told stories

made him a very delightful acquaintance; he was always so agreeable and witty that he was called by his most intimate friends the "Laughing Philosopher", and it seems to me that the term "Epicurean Philosopher", which I have often heard applied to him, describes him accurately and briefly. In public business my grandfather was upright and honourable; but as he advanced in years his detestation of anything disagreeable made him simply avoid whatever fretted him, laughing off all sorts of ordinary calls upon his leisure time. His love of ease and kindness of heart made it impossible that he could be actively unkind to any one, but he would not be worried, and just got away from anything that annoyed him. He was very fond of his children, and was an indulgent father to them, and he was a kind and affectionate grandfather; he could not bear any one to be unhappy or uncomfortable about him, and this feeling he carried down the animal creation; his pet cats and dogs were especially cared for by himself, the birds in the garden were carefully watched over and fed, and no gun was ever allowed to be fired about the place. After he retired from the India House he seldom left Halliford; his life was spent among his books, and in the garden, in which he took great pleasure, and on the river. May-day he always kept in true old English fashion; all the children of the village came round with their garlands of flowers, and each child was presented with a new penny, or silver threepenny or four-penny piece, according to the beauty of their garlands; the money was given by the Queen of the May, always one of his granddaughters, who sat beside him, dressed in white and crowned with flowers, and holding a sceptre of flowers in her hand.

He was, indeed, a fine, genial, occasionally irritable, autocratic, bookish and epicurean old gentleman, as full of crotchets and as ripe a character as any of the figures in his own pages. We are told that one evening two men from the neighbourhood were rowing down the river, and as they passed the house, one of them, not certain of his bearings, asked the other: "Is this old

Peacock's?" Immediately there came a thundering
reply from the garden: "Yes, this is old Peacock's,
and this is old Peacock." We know how he measured
the height of the river and noted the changes of the
weather, how he was so afraid of fire that he would
only allow his household a few matches and would not
tolerate smoking (which he hated for several reasons)
anywhere on his premises, how he would have nothing
to do with afternoon tea because, he declared, it spoilt
dinner, how he ordered dinner every day himself and
made of that meal, with its accompanying libations, a
very stately affair indeed. To the end of his days, he
read hard, mostly in Greek (though he discovered Dickens
during the last year of his life and delighted in
him), and his sight was so good that he never even
wore spectacles. There was nothing phenomenal in his
length of life, yet it is strange to think of him still
thumbing his Aristophanes and drinking his Madeira
in the 'sixties. Because so many of his famous contemporaries died young, he, like Landor and Leigh Hunt,
seems to have lived in two entirely different worlds,
to have survived a deluge. To younger men of letters
—and unfortunately only one or two ever caught sight
of him—Peacock must have seemed almost a figure from
mythology. We know what one of them thought,
for Robert Buchanan, shortly after he arrived in London, called on Peacock and afterwards described his visit.
He found the old novelist seated on his garden
lawn in the sun, with little Clari Leigh Hunt by
his knee. This child herself was a curious link with
the past, for she was the granddaughter of both Leigh
Hunt and the Williams who was drowned with Shelley.
Buchanan writes:

And this old man had spoken with Shelley not once but a thousand times, and had known well both Harriet Westbrook and Mary Godwin; and had cracked jokes with Hobhouse, and chaffed Proctor's latinity; and had seen, and actually criticised, Malibran; and had bought "the vasty version of a new system to perplex the sages" (Byron's description of Wordsworth's *Excursion*), when it first came out, in a bright, new, uncut quarto; and had dined with Jeremy Bentham; and had smiled at Disraeli, when, resplendently attired, he stood chatting at Hookham's with the Countess of Blessington; and had been face to face with that bland Rhadamanthus, Chief Justice Eldon; and was, in short, such a living chronicle of things past and men dead as filled one's soul with delight and ever-varying wonder.

Peacock had done all this and more, and now there was but one thing left for him to do. For some time he had been possessed by what seemed to his household an absurd or perhaps morbid dread of fire, and curiously enough it was an actual outbreak of fire, in the roof of his bedroom, that hastened his end. He could not help to put out the fire, but when he was urged to leave the house and take shelter at a neigh- bour's, we are told that he stoutly refused, shouting, "By the immortal gods, I will not move!" His house and treasures were saved, but now he was compelled to take to his bed. This was late in 1865. In the New Year he began to suffer from intestinal cramps, and his granddaughter has recorded how, towards the end, she would hear him calling upon the immortal gods and reproaching them because they tormented so old and faithful a servant. He died on January 23, 1866, and was buried in the New Cemetery at Shepperton.

When Peacock was a little boy, he was so notice- ably good-looking, we are told, that Queen Charlotte, passing him on the road, stopped her carriage to give him a kiss. He grew up to be—in his granddaughter's word's—

A fine tall, handsome man, with a profusion of bright, brown hair, eyes of fine dark blue, massive brow, and regular features, a Roman nose, a handsome mouth, which, when he laughed, as I well remember, turned up at the corners, and a complexion, fair as a girl's; his hair was peculiar in its wild luxuriant growth, it seemed to grow all from the top of his head, had no parting, but hung about in thick locks with a rich wave all through it, and as an old man, it turned to that beautiful bright silver-white, which one so seldom sees; at his death, in his eighty-first year, it was as profuse in quantity as when he was a young man.

There is a portrait of him, as he was in later life, by Henry Wallis, hanging in the National Portrait Gallery. It shows us a man with a strong, handsome face, at once rather rubicund and severe, but the general handling of the portrait does not inspire confidence. Much better is the photograph taken, much against his will, in 1857 when he was seventy-two. The face is framed in thick white hair; the eyes, under heavy brows, are shrewd and kindly; and there is infinite humour in the long upper lip and the mouth. Here, it is evident, is the man we know in the novels.

Already we have made the acquaintance of his very decided tastes. All his life he delighted in walking and boating. In his youth, as we have seen, he went to Scotland, and spent some happy months roaming about the Welsh mountains, but after he had reached early manhood he would seem to have lost all desire for travel. It is significant that he should have lived quite contentedly in one place for the greater part of his life. Lower Halliford suited him and so he remained there, dividing his time between the library, the garden and the river. There never was a man, it would appear, with less desire for novelty of any kind than Peacock. Very early in life he seems to have made up his mind that certain things would give him all the pleasure he wanted, and ever afterwards we find him serenely enjoying those things. This is well illustrated by his taste in books. He was, as we have seen, a hard reader for two-thirds of a century, and was familiar with five literatures, Greek, Latin, English, French and Italian. In his old age he added a sixth, Spanish. In addition, he had made some study of Welsh. With German he would have nothing to do, probably because he heartily disliked the German philosophy and ultra-romantic poetry, drama and fiction, that were so fashionable in his youth. There is here sufficient breadth of scholarship, but his own personal tastes were comparatively narrow. He soon discovered what he wanted and thereafter was not inclined to make experiments. His favourites he read over and over again. These were Homer, Sophocles, Aristophanes and Nonnus, whose *Dionysiaca* he called "the finest poem in the world after the *Iliad*", but was not unaware of the fact that most of his hearers had never set eyes on it; Virgil, Horace, Cicero, Petronius and Tacitus, who undoubtedly had an influence upon his own style; Pulci, Ariosto, Bojardo, among the Italians, and Rabelais and Voltaire among the French. His English favourites were probably Shakespeare, Chaucer and the author of Hudibras, but perhaps it is hardly fair to single out these or any other three writers because his taste in English literature was fairly catholic, more so than one would at first imagine. It is easy to understand his pleasure in the Restoration dramatists and the Augustan wits, but his judgment of contemporary literature is rather surprising. Thus, in spite of his persistent mockery, he had a genuine appreciation of Wordsworth and Coleridge as poets. He saw the weakness of Byron and Byronism, but he admired Byron's best work and could be enthusiastic over *Don Juan.* He has been accused of being indifferent to Shelley's genius, but a glance at the *Memoirs,* in which the nature of that genius is admirably described, will show that there is no truth in the charge. Indeed, when we consider the difference in temperament and point of view, we must admit that his appreciation of all these poets, who were contemporaries, to be liked or disliked at will, and not great figures in some past golden age, proves that at times his purely literary judgment was so good that it frequently got the better of him, for undoubtedly he would have found it more convenient to have disliked all contemporary Romantics. This he contrived to do with Keats and Tennyson, whom he dismissed with pedantic quibbles. On the other hand, if he sometimes mistook a swan for a goose, he never fell into the opposing error of mistaking geese for swans: the Campbells and Tom Moores and Barry Cornwalls never received any of Peacock's suffrages.

It is, however, his attitude towards the great writers of the past that reveals the man. That list of favourite authors already quoted is significant. A list of those authors, of equal stature, who were not to his taste, would be equally significant, and such a list would probably include such massive figures as Euripides, Lucretius, Dante, Milton. As Buchanan remarked:

"His sympathies, indeed, were less with the grand, the terrible, and the sublimely pathetic, than with the brilliant, the exquisite, and the delicately artistic". The adjectives are none too well chosen, but we shall not quarrel with the judgment. Peacock's tastes were obviously those of a humanist. Mysticism he disliked, and even an intense moral earnestness left him uncomfortable. He was not one of those persons who feel that they are spirits exiled here for a season. He did not see this world as a place cloudy with doom or this life as a brief and bitter trial. He turns aside even from the satirists if their voices are too harsh and their laughter too embittered, and we do not find Juvenal and Swift among his chosen companions. He looks in literature for laughter and sunlight and ease, gracious forms and pleasant green places, roaring farce or light keen mockery, human relations that are droll or affectionate, touched with tenderness but undisturbed by deep passion, all going their way beneath the fair sky of good sense.

Peacock has been unfortunate in appearing before the reading public so frequently as a figure in the various biographies of his friend Shelley. There, as he coolly strolls through one perfervid chapter after another, he is apt to seem a very cold and supercilious person. Many Shelley enthusiasts, who, unlike their idol, have not been able to escape from *Nightmare Abbey* and to laugh at the antics there, have made no secret of their dislike for the creator of Scythrop. Other people, more detached, have yet been influenced in their attitude towards Peacock, as a man if not as a writer, by vague memories of a detached shrugging figure in the brief shining chronicle of Shelley's life.

Even so fine a critic as Richard Garnett, for example, who clearly rejoices in the task of praising the writer, immediately cools when he turns to the man. It is difficult to avoid the suspicion that the critic is involuntarily seeing Peacock against the background of Shelley's life. Peacock did not love humanity and die young. Peacock laughed at humanity, made himself snug, and could still be discovered sipping his port and Madeira when he was eighty. This contrast, making itself felt somewhere at the back of the mind, has been too compelling for many critics. But there are other reasons, too, why Peacock as a man should irritate, if not actually repel, so many critics and students of literature. To begin with, there was in him not a little of the amateur, not the eager appealing amateur but the disdainful aristocratic amateur of letters, who writes for his own pleasure and shows no particular anxiety to be commended for what he has done. There is about such men an air of self-sufficiency that is vaguely irritating. And Peacock was peculiarly self-sufficient both as a writer and a man. If he had misfortunes, he kept them to himself; he made no demand whatever upon public sympathy; he appeared to be for ever cool and comfortable. His poetry seemed the occasional indulgence of a scholar and gentleman; his fiction, for the most part published anonymously, was not unlike a domestic joke; and his official life, in which he was apparently very efficient, very successful, was almost entirely hidden from the public view. Such independence is not altogether to our taste. Not only are we robbed of any opportunity for indulging in posthumous pity, one of the pleasantest and cheapest of emotions, but we are not even favoured with the usual demand for our suffrages.

Thus, retiring somewhat baffled, we cannot help feeling that the man was too successful, too comfortable: hence the cool references to him, the talk of "self-indulgence", as if all critics and readers were fasting friars.

At this point it would be well to glance at some facts of his life and some of his more obvious characteristics. He was fond of ease and comfort and good living, and as he grew older "his detestation of anything disagreeable made him simply avoid whatever fretted him, laughing off all sorts of ordinary calls upon his leisure time". This type of elderly man, touched with a genial selfishness, is not unfamiliar. But Peacock was obviously free from the grosser forms of selfishness, and such egoism as his was frank and open, humorously paraded, and not, as egoism so often is, subtly disguised, hidden away, to gnaw at the roots of his character. We know that in his public business he was upright and honourable. His more serious convictions were honestly arrived at, tenaciously held, and courageously expressed. He was Shelley's friend during the time when it was not very convenient nor even safe to act in that capacity. It is true that he was under obligations to Shelley, but so were a great many other people who all contrived to be missing when the poet most needed sympathy and help. Years later, as we have seen, Peacock sturdily defended Harriet's memory and drew down upon himself the wrath of those who were busy fighting Shelley's battles for him at a remove of forty years. And whatever views, progressive or reactionary, Peacock put forward, they were never the easy fashionable ones. Shelley admired him in his youth, and Meredith admired him in his old age.

Men like Thackeray and Macaulay enjoyed his company and would have been glad to have had more of it. There is no evidence that he ever lost a friend, a significant fact; and if he would seem to have had few friends it is merely because he never asked for more. There is a familiar type of public man who has such an intense love of humanity in general that he has no affection left for human beings in particular, and frequently contrives to wreck the happiness of all the people near him, his charity beginning anywhere but at home. Peacock belongs to the opposing type. He makes no pretence of loving everybody, but he did really care for the human beings nearest to him, who may have had to submit to a few whims and little pieces of self-indulgence, but whose lives were never ruined by any egoistical pranks of his. He was a good son, a good husband, and a good father, not simply coldly dutiful, but tender and affectionate. He appears to the mind's eye probably as he would have wished to appear, as a figure of easy prosperity, a laughing philosopher against a background of gardens and libraries and tables shining with old silver and decanters. But in his private life he was sorely tried by fortune: his favourite child died when she was three; his wife became an invalid; his eldest daughter was quickly widowed and then made her tragic marriage with Meredith; his son was unstable and a constant source of anxiety; his youngest daughter lost her two children and died herself not long afterwards; few men have known more misfortunes in their domestic life. The man who wrote *Gryll Grange,* around which some of these tragic events are grouped, must have had a brave heart or a very unfeeling one, and we have ample testimony that Peacock was anything but insensitive.

We have called him self-sufficient, and undoubtedly it was his desire, within the limits of an affectionate nature, to be self-sufficient. Unlike a familiar type of author, who is very vain but not at all proud, ready to do almost anything for a little applause, Peacock was very proud but not at all vain. His lack of vanity explains the curious anonymity of his life and works. Few writers have shown themselves less eager for praise or even common recognition. But if this is explained by his lack of vanity, it is also explained by his pride, which made him stand apart and not compete, and turned his authorship into a gentlemanly whim. Once he had passed his early youth, when fortune gave him several hard buffets (the greatest of them the tragic conclusion of his first love affair, which left a deep impression) Peacock wished to be always a little detached from life, to be always master of circumstance. In addition, as we have seen, he reacted almost violently from the ultra-romantic tendencies that he observed in Shelley and his set and in so much of the literature of the period, in which characters drifted helplessly on the tide of passion and changing mood. The fact that he had for a time played this character himself, and not with any conspicuous literary success, only hastened this reaction. Nevertheless, as one or two astute critics have noticed, he always remained a Romantic at heart. People who see him as nothing but the spokesman of common sense have mistaken their man, just as those who regard him mainly as a political satirist (on their own side of the question) have mistaken their man. In this they have been helped by

Peacock himself. He chose for his seal the Horatian
line: *Nec tardum opperior nec praecedentibus insto*.
This is how he liked to see himself, as a cool, moderate
man, occupying a sensible middle position. But in
his heart of hearts, he knew he was nothing of the kind
and may often be found, in the curious fashion of his
type, laughing at himself. His very courtship and
marriage were as whimsical as anything in his novels,
and there is hardly anybody in *Crotchet Castle* more
crotchety than its author. As for his politics and
political satire, they will be discussed later; it is only
necessary here to point out that they are so odd that
he can be claimed by all political parties with some
show of reason and by none with complete justice.
All these simple explanations of his character are superficial, and the slightest critical examination of his work
will demonstrate how inadequate they are fully to
account for it. It asks us to look for a more complicated character with a tangle of motives. Like
every humorist who is something more than a mere
joker, Peacock was really a secret and baffled idealist.
He laughed at the world because it was incongruous
and droll, and he saw it was incongruous and droll
because he had compared it with another and better
world, hidden away in his dream. His extraordinary
passion for Greek is in part explained by the fact that
it enabled him to escape into what seemed to him an
ideal world.

There is nothing of the true realistic temper in his
works. Even their astonishing conviviality is an idealisation. Even their love passages, which do not play
an important part but would be more important to himself and his contemporary readers than they are to us,

who find them stilted and perfunctory, bear witness to
the idealist in him. His novels laugh at most things,
but they do not laugh at love, and he did not fill them
with happy young lovers to please the novel-reading public, for which he cared not a rap, but to please
himself. Indeed, his satire is never directed against
what we might call private life. This was clearly seen
by Raleigh, who has left us a tiny chapter on Peacock in a posthumously published volume of notes. This
chapter exaggerates one side of Peacock's character,
but Raleigh's opening remarks are extraordinarily
penetrating:

There is nothing misanthropical about Peacock. He
admires, and loves. All that is simple and matter of
affection, and private, is dear to him. He laughs at
idealists, and makers of systems. Yet—here is the strange
thing—he is not common sense against the idea. He has,
deep down in him, a great love for ideas. How easy to
make fun of Rousseau, Mme. de Genlis, Thomas Day—all
that world of theory which belongs to the French Revolution! Peacock does make fun of it, but he has been touched
by it.

The rest of the passage should be read, though Raleigh
goes wrong in places, chiefly because he argues too
much from *Melincourt,* which in some respects, as we
have already seen, is not typical of its author. But
Raleigh touches Peacock's secret when he indicates
briefly (the above are notes that were verbally expanded
in lectures) Peacock's attitude towards ideas. If Peacock had cared nothing for ideas, had been the servant
of downright common sense that some of his critics
imagine him to have been, he would never have
taken the trouble to explore ideas so thoroughly, would
never have studied the hundred and one authors he

quotes in his footnotes and parodies in his text. The
truth is that he was at once attracted and repelled by
those large simple philosophic theories and systems
that were the mental diet of Godwin and his circle or
the Bracknell set. The crank or crotcheteer is his prey
not because he himself is far removed from one but
because he himself only just stops short of being one.
Indeed, he has his own crotchets. His mind, like
Shelley's, lived in the kingdom of philosophic theories
and systems and ideals, and if Shelley was its bard,
Peacock was its Court Jester. It is this position, as
the comedian of the life of ideas, that makes Peacock a
unique figure in English Literature.

We shall see later, when we come to examine his
fiction, what use he made of this position. We have
first to discover—and the inquiry is pertinent to any
discussion of his character—how he came to hold such
a position. Perhaps the best line of approach will be
a comparison and contrast with his friend, Shelley.
We think of them representing two different halves of
humanity. There never was, at first sight, such a
piquant association. But when we begin to consider
their personalities and their relation more closely, we
discover that they are not so sharply opposed as we
first imagined. We remember that Peacock could be
influenced by Shelley, that Shelley could admire Peacock. And probably there was a time, during the
first year or so of their friendship, when the likeness between them would be far more apparent than the
difference. They shared a passion for certain pursuits;
they were both in rebellion against conventional thought
and belief; they were both romantic and idealistic.
We can imagine them for a time keeping step together.

But very soon their ways diverge, until at last they have
almost lost sight of one another. In this matter of
idealism, it might be said that Shelley was bold and
Peacock was shy. Shelley had intensity, could easily
kindle his imagination into a blaze, and had the faculty
of believing what he wanted to believe and seeing what
he wanted to see. Peacock, cooler, with an exquisite
sense of proportion (which is of course precisely what
is lacking in all cranks and crotcheteers) that forced the
ludicrous upon his attention, was inevitably compelled
to be more detached. He could not possibly hurl his
whole mind in one direction as Shelley could. His
sense of humour was for ever warning his pride that he
was about to make a fool of himself. He could not
accept the world and he could not begin to mend it;
he could not help being drawn to the idealists and
makers of systems and he could not help discovering
how inadequate they were; he could not fall out of love
with ideas and yet he could not marry them; thus he
was left, a Mahomet's coffin, in mid-air. So situated,
a man must either laugh or be laughed at, so Peacock
laughed. By his laughter he doubly revenged himself
on a world that he could not accept and reformers
he could not join: he mocked the complacency of a
world that imagined itself to be in no need of reforma-
tion, and equally mocked the complacency of those
who thought they were capable of reforming it. His
singular position left his energetic and powerful mind
without proportionate objects on which to fasten, and
inevitably it sought relief, outside scholarship, in wit
and intellectual mischief, soaring into sheer high
spirits. He became the playboy of the intellectual
world.

LATER LIFE AND CHARACTER

Both he and Shelley wished to escape from the present, but when they did escape they turned different ways. Shelley jumped forward into the future. Peacock returned to the past, but not to the real past, but to some golden age of classic myth and poetry. He knew himself that it was not the real past; but this little dream world, filled with unenclosed forests and quiet gardens, pure air, food and liquor, a fit habitation for poets and philosophers and fair women, concretely represented the good life, whatever Peacock could solidly accept, and thus served as a basis for sardonic comparison with the present world. And his Epicureanism is not unconnected with this pretended belief in a past that never existed. It must not be taken too seriously, for it is largely an attitude, part mischievous, part defensive. Feeling compelled, at times, to make some affirmative gesture, Peacock played the pagan. But when a blow really fell, he dropped the part and retired until the wound healed and he was ready to laugh again. We know how, when his favourite child died so suddenly, he said to his friend Strachey: "There are times when the world cannot be made fun of." A tragedy is being played simultaneously with the comedy of this life. There is something in Peacock's remark that suggests that he liked to pretend to himself that the tragedy, with which he did not know how to cope, was not really there, until there came a time when it forced itself upon him and he could pretend no longer. The Friar's famous speech, in *Maid Marian,* beginning: "The world is a stage, and life is a farce, and he that laughs most has most profit of the performance," does not apply to a world that contains the deaths of little children. Peacock's philosophy

was an excellent one for fine afternoons in the
garden and untroubled evenings in the library, enabling
him to endure the occasional trials of a corked wine
and a mislaid folio; but it would be as useful to a man
really grappling with this life as a toy whip would
be to a lion-tamer. All this would be very damaging if Peacock made any pretence of being a serious
interpreter of life, but he made no such pretence and
only begged leave to make fun of the world. He
kept his troubles to himself, but liberally shared his
pleasures. His laughter is not harsh, misanthropical,
a revenge for joys left untasted. His humour is like a
ripe old sherry, dry yet genial, with sunshine in the
heart of it.

CHAPTER V

HIS POETRY

IT might be said of Peacock that he achieved poetry only when he had ceased to be a poet. As we have seen, he began as a poet and wrote nothing but verse until he was past thirty, when he produced *Headlong Hall* in 1816. After that he takes his place in letters as a prose man, but a prose man who can never resist a lyrical impulse and who does not hesitate to introduce a large number of songs, sentimental and convivial, into his satirical novels. Thus he becomes an occasional poet and in this capacity he succeeds beyond a doubt. But when, earlier, he had attempted poetry alone, had essayed the grand manner, his failure was even more marked than his later success. There is just one period, which gave us *Rhododaphne,* his long and not unambitious narrative poem, when he seems to occupy a middle position, having turned novelist and occasional poet and yet not having relinquished the rôle of poet proper, but this fact does not greatly disturb our argument. *Rhododaphne* is certainly not a failure, but it cannot compare, in interest, originality, in all the qualities that make for survival in literature, with either his novels or the best of his short lyrics. Admirable as the poem is, there is nothing in it to suggest that Peacock was mistaken in following his satirical and humorous bent in prose and simply satisfying an occasional lyrical impulse. Perhaps it would not be an exaggeration to say that his prose saved his poetry, for it supplied him with a major instrument and left him free to give us what Richard Garnett (somewhat too admiringly) calls those "gushes and snatches of song almost birdlike in their sweetness and simplicity".

His early verse does not suggest a possible future for him even as an occasional poet, if we except one short lyric, *The Grave of Love,* of uncertain date. It provides us with typical specimens of that tepid versifying which now serves only as a dim background for the blazing splendour of the new Romantic poetry, the work of Wordsworth, Coleridge, Shelley, Keats, Byron. It is written in what is probably the worst, the feeblest and dullest, traditional manner that we have had in English Poetry, worse than the equivalent traditional manner, slap-dash, fantastic, foppish, laboured, of the sixteenth, seventeenth and eighteenth centuries respectively. The last decade of the eighteenth century and the first twenty years of the nineteenth produced an enormous quantity of this kind of verse, in which the writer timidly exploits a romantic mood, but neither honestly examines his own mind nor tries to express his real emotions, and describes everything in such a way as to drain all colour and bloom and character and life out of it, leaving it vague, unreal, abstract. Lord Houghton, discussing Peacock's early poems, remarks very truly that they belong to a time

when verse-writing was a gentleman-like recreation as well as a divine afflatus, and when a critic no more thought

of dissecting a pleasant piece of rhyme than a man of science
would object to the deficient mechanism of the toys of
childhood. They are full of that imagery which transformed the affections and mental faculties into mythological
personages, and haunted all nature with a new and uninter-
esting polytheism, while it established a certain obligatory
diction for verse, that now sounds intolerably forced and
pedantic. . . .

Any person wishing to make the acquaintance of that
"obligatory diction for verse" cannot do better than to
turn to Peacock's early poems. In these, as usual, the
poet, with his *lay* and his *numbers, roves* through
smiling plains, o'er mountains dreary, on *desolate shores,*
or *lightly springs* to meet some *matchless nymph* in some
fair bower, attended by the *sylvan muses* and the *genial
rays* of the sun, and his *thoughts are beguil'd* by *visions
wild* because he is *creative Fancy's child,* and at once
the victim of *dark Despair* and the pupil of *inspiring
Hope.*

Peacock's two long poems, *Palmyra* and *The Genius
of the Thames,* are typical productions of this method
of versifying. In the first there are more footnotes
than verse, and all that the poet can do to improve
upon the honest impressive records of the travellers and
historians he quotes is to indulge in the most reckless
personification:

> Enthusiast FANCY, rob'd in light,
> Pours on the air her many sparkling rays,
> Redeeming from OBLIVION's deep'ning night
>   The deeds of ancient days.
>   The mighty forms of chiefs of old,
> To VIRTUE dear, and PATRIOT TRUTH sublime,
>   In feeble splendour I behold,
> Discover'd dimly through the mists of TIME,
> As through the vapours of the mountain-stream
> With pale reflection glows the sun's declining beam.

And by also indulging in the most lofty moralising at
every other turn—

> The noblest works of human pow'r
> In vain resist the fate-fraught hour;
> The marble hall, the rock-built tow'r,
>   Alike submit to destiny:
> OBLIVION's awful storms resound;
> The massy columns fall around;
> The fabric totters to the ground,
>   And darkness veils its memory!

he hopes to make the reader overlook the fact that he,
the poet, has never set eyes on the place and is in reality
completely unmoved by its fate, being merely glad of
an excuse for a little high-falutin' in rhyme. The greater
part of the poem gives us history in which such personages as DESTRUCTION, wild CONFUSION, with'ring
DREAD, and stern DESPAIR are the principal actors.
The Genius of the Thames is a more ambitious performance. Here the poet is writing about something he
knows, but that does not prevent his giving us a large
number of footnotes. Thus the line "Where Nile's mysterious sources sleep" is accompanied by a note stating
that "Bruce penetrated to the source of the eastern branch
of the Nile: that of the western, which is the principal
branch, has never yet been visited by an European".
Indeed, there is here a good deal of valuable information about the Thames, which the poet solemnly traces
from source to mouth, and about various other rivers;
and the verses are inspired by an unexceptionable spirit of
patriotism:

> Throned in Augusta's ample port,
> Imperial commerce holds her court,
>   And Britain's power sublimes:
> To her the breath of every breeze
> Conveys the wealth of subject seas,
>   And tributary climes.

> Adventurous courage guides the helm
> From every port of every realm:
> Through gales that rage, and waves that whelm,
>   Unnumbered vessels ride:
> Till all their various ensigns fly,
> Beneath Britannia's milder sky,
> Where roves, oh Thames! the patriot's eye
>   O'er thy refulgent tide.

Here is the patriot's eye indeed, but not the poet's eye in fine frenzy rolling. And we may amuse ourselves imagining what Peacock's comment on such verses as these would have been if they had been brought to his notice for the first time a little later in life. The poem is undoubtedly based on the best models; all the necessary information, topographical, historical, biographical, is there, together with all the appropriate comment; but it is all dead versifying and nowhere does the poet catch fire, light up his lines with passion (and, after all, he had a passion for this river and it remained with him to the end of his life), or strike out vivid and memorable phrases. Here is the river but no genius, the Thames but not the Thames on fire.

It is significant that many of the shorter poems of this period are either translations or imitations. There is more evidence here of the scholar, sensitive to fine literature and given to exercising himself occasionally in the making of verse, than there is of the ardent full creative poetic mind, to which Peacock had little claim then or later. He does not even pour out those floods of nonsense that better and bigger poets have given us in their nonage. He is clearly a somewhat timid and tepid verse-maker who does not feel any strong impulse to express himself. Even his amatory verses seem like exercises. Thus he begins his *Farewell to Matilda* with—

> Matilda, farewell! Fate has doom'd us to part,
> But the prospect occasions no pang to my heart;
> No longer is love with my reason at strife,
> Though once thou wert dearer, far dearer than life.

And even a later lyric, which has probably more personal feeling behind it, *Remember Me*, seems quite cold:

> And what are life's enchanting dreams,
>   That melt, like morning mists, away?
> And what are Fancy's golden beams,
>   That glow with transitory day?
> While adverse stars my steps impel,
>   To climes remote, my love, from thee,
> Will that dear breast with pity swell,
>   And wilt thou still remember me?

Our sympathy is not to be bought by such common worn coinage of versifying. There is, however, one exception, a lyric in which strong personal feeling has at last found memorable expression. This is the little poem, inspired by his first tragic love affair, *The Grave of Love*:

> I dug, beneath the cypress shade,
>   What well might seem an elfin's grave;
> And every pledge in earth I laid,
>   That erst thy false affection gave.
>
> I pressed them down the sod beneath;
>   I placed one mossy stone above;
> And twined the rose's fading wreath
>   Around the sepulchre of love.
>
> Frail as thy love, the flowers were dead
>   Ere yet the evening sun was set:
> But years shall see the cypress spread,
>   Immutable as my regret.

It is not faultless—there is a certain shade of artificiality, a faint tinsel glitter, about the language, at least in the first two verses and especially in the fourth line—but it is very beautifully turned and the last verse is a triumph. It is the first poem of any importance that he wrote, and it is characteristic of him at his best. There is here no lyrical intensity, no great cry, no sudden flight of the imagination; it is the poetry, we feel, of a prose mind, something between pure song and wit, the lyrical touched with the epigrammatic, reminding us of Landor, though less chiselled and more graceful. Thus we cannot accept the critic's "snatches of song almost birdlike in their sweetness and simplicity", for the artless, effortless loveliness of the purely lyrical poet, trilling as easily as a bird, will not be found in Peacock, who is always conscious, deliberate, delicately sophisticated even when he appears at his simplest.

Peacock's longest and most ambitious poem was, of course, *Rhododaphne,* which, as we have already seen, was very greatly admired in its own day and received the praises of Shelley, Byron and Poe. Since that day it has perhaps been somewhat neglected and underestimated. But we cannot in strict justice complain that it has been very unfairly neglected nor grossly under-estimated, for though, after a cool summary of its qualities, it would appear to lack very little, the little that it does lack is all-important. It is not a poem that demands to be read again and again; it just fails to take root in a reader's imagination; it wants those great moments in which a poet seems to burst through into an inner and more intense reality, when words are oracular and magical and spell a vision. Moreover, to descend a little, though it makes innumerable charming pictures, flashing bright clear imagery past the reader's inward eye, it is neither sharp and exact enough, on the one hand, nor sufficiently bold and suggestive, on the other, to leave us with the sense of having gone through an experience ourselves. Reading it is like watching a stream glide past. Lacking the highest qualities, the poem might as well lack everything meritorious in poetry so far as our own time is concerned, if only because the narrative poem itself has largely fallen into disfavour with us and only the supreme poetic appeal will conquer our prejudice against this form of the art. A hundred years ago the narrative poem was in high favour, and therefore it is not surprising that *Rhododaphne* should have been praised so widely and by such good judges. It is not surprising simply because the poem has solid merit and is, indeed, an excellent specimen of its kind. To begin with, it is a narrative poem that has a genuine narrative. It really does succeed in telling the tale it sets out to tell, which is more than can be said of some far more famous narrative poems. Again, it is one of the few poems dealing with the ancient classical world that really do seem to be animated by the spirit of that world. In reading it we do not feel that we are attending a masquerade. We may not feel that we are actually living *in* that world—for as we have seen it is the weakness of the poem that it does not compel us to share an experience—but we do at least feel that we are looking at it from afar, that it is spread there before us, bright and clear.

It shows us the most romantic aspect of that ancient world, for it is filled with that strange Thessalian magic which we find in Apuleius. It tells how Anthemion, the flower of all Arcadia's youth, came to the Temple of Love at Thespia, to pray for his beloved Calliroë, who was wasting away; and how he met the beautiful

enchantress Rhododaphne, who sought his love and by
her arts seemed to bring about the death of Calliroë;
and how, after many adventures, Anthemion and Rhododaphne lived together in a palace of enchant-
ment, until at last her power wanes and she is killed by
the statue of Uranian Love, and Calliroë, awakening
from a magic sleep, is restored to her lover. The octosyl-
labic lines ran easily and swiftly and are crowded with
bright imagery. The poem has a certain clarity and profusion of light that suggest the morning of the world.
It is filled with charming little pictures:

> He bore a simple wild-flower wreath:
> Narcissus, and the sweet-briar rose;
> Vervain, and flexile thyme, that breathe
> Rich fragrance; modest heath, that glows
> With purple bells; the amaranth bright,
> That no decay nor fading knows . . .

Or this, from the inset tale of Bacchus and the Pirates:

> While he speaks, and fiercely tightens
> In the full free breeze the sail,
> From the deck wine bubbling lightens,
> Winy fragrance fills the gale.
> Gurgling in ambrosial lustre
> Flows the purple-eddying wine:
> O'er the yard-arms trail and cluster
> Tendrils of the mantling vine:
> Grapes, beneath the broad leaves springing,
> Blushing as in vintage-hours,
> Droop, while round the tall mast clinging
> Ivy twines its buds and flowers,
> Fast with graceful berries blackening:
> Garlands hang on every oar:
> Then in fear the cordage slackening,
> One and all, they cry, "To shore!"
> Bacchus changed his shape, and glaring
> With a lion's eye-balls wide,
> Roared: the pirate-crew, despairing,
> Plunged amid the foaming tide.
> Through the azure depths they flitted
> Dolphins by transforming fate. . . .

And, in spite of a certain cloying sweetness and
monotonous glitter in the language, there is real beauty
in his description of the life of Anthemion and Rhododaphne in her enchanted palace, where

> Maids with silver flasks advancing,
> Pour the wine's red-sparkling tide,
> Which youth, with heads recumbent dancing,
> Catch in goblets as they glide:
> All upon the odorous air
> Lightly toss their leafy hair. . . .

But the finest passages in the poem are those in which
the poet ceases to be a narrator and speaks in his own
person, being moved by a feeling of regret at the thought
of this lost world:

> By living streams, in sylvan shades,
> Where winds and waves symphonious make
> Sweet melody, the youths and maids
> No more with coral music wake
> Lone Echo from her tangled brake,
> On Pan, or Sylvan Genius, calling,
> Naiad or Nymph, in suppliant song:
> No more by living fountain, falling
> The poplar's circling bower among,
> Where pious hands have carved of yore
> Rude bason for its lucid store
> And reared the grassy altar nigh,
> The traveller, when the sun ride high,
> For cool refreshment lingering there,
> Pours to the Sister Nymphs his prayer.
> Yet still the green vales smile: the springs
> Gush forth in light: the forest weaves
> Its own wild bowers; the breeze's wings
> Make music in their rustling leaves;
> But 'tis no spirit's breath that sighs
> Among their tangled canopies;
> In ocean's caves no Nereid dwells:
> No Oread walks the mountain-dells:
> The streams no sedge-crowned Genii roll
> From bounteous urn: great Pan is dead:
> The life, the intellectual soul
> Of vale, and grove, and stream, has fled
> For ever with the creed sublime
> That nursed the Muse of earlier time.

There is an increased power in these lines because the familiar sentiment they express is, for once, something really felt by the poet and not merely part of a conveniently picturesque and sentimental attitude. Peacock is here writing out of his pagan heart. There is a companion passage in which he is perhaps even more successful in reaching what is for him the rare height of pure romantic poetry:

> Magic and mystery, spells Circæan,
> The Siren voice, that calmed the sea,
> And steeped the soul in dews Lethæan;
> The enchanted chalice, sparkling free
> With wine, amid whose ruby glow
> Love couched, with madness linked and woe;
> Mantle and zone, whose woof beneath
> Lurked wily grace, in subtle wreath
> With blandishment and young desire
> And soft persuasion intertwined,
> Whose touch, with sympathetic fire,
> Could melt at once the sternest mind;
> Have passed away: for vestal truth
> Young Fancy's foe, and Reason chill,
> Have chased the dreams that charmed the youth
> Of nature and the world, which still,
> Amid that vestal light severe,
> Our colder spirits leap to hear
> Like echoes from a fairy hill. . . .

Even in these passages, it will be noticed, he never quite succeeds in purging his style of those hackneyed conventional usages of verse, that "obligatory diction" and frigid personification, which are so characteristic of his early poems. There is the author of *Palmyra* or *The Genius of the Thames* in such a line as "Young Fancy's foe, and Reason chill". But there is a touch of Keatsian magic in "Like echoes from a fairy hill", just as there is more than a suggestion of Wordsworthian grandeur in the concluding lines of the first passage, the lines beginning "Great Pan is dead"; and if there had only been one canto out of the seven that make up *Rhododaphne* on this height, there would have been a very different story to tell of Peacock, and this chapter would have been considerably enlarged.

The rest of his work in verse consists of short lyrics, and most of these found their way into his novels as songs and ballads, sentimental or convivial. There are, however, two notable exceptions, both little personal lyrics. The first is the little poem he wrote for the tombstone of his daughter, Margaret, who died at the age of three in 1826:

> Long night succeeds thy little day;
>   Oh blighted blossom! can it be,
> That this grey stone and grassy clay
>   Have closed our anxious care of thee?
>
> The half-form'd speech of artless thought
>   That spoke a mind beyond thy years;
> The song, the dance, by nature taught;
>   The sunny smiles, the transient tears;
>
> The symmetry of face and form,
>   The eye with light and life replete;
> The little heart so fondly warm;
>   The voice so musically sweet.
>
> Those lost to hope, in memory yet
>   Around the hearts that lov'd thee cling,
> Shadowing, with long and vain regret,
>   The too fair promise of thy spring.

And the second is the poem he wrote in 1842, *Newark Abbey*, out of the memory of his first love, the poem that Tennyson admired, beginning:

> I gaze where August's sunbeam falls
> Along these grey and lonely walls,
> Till in its light absorbed appears
> The lapse of five-and-thirty years. . . .

in which simple opening lines there is a curious
poignancy that the remainder of the poem, with its
deliberate sentimental musing, hardly reaches. There
is nothing else on this level outside the songs from the
novels, and these songs are of course quite different
in character.

A large number of these lyrics would serve admirably
as words for music—and most of them, of course, are
actually supposed to be sung in the novels—but are of
no great interest if regarded as independent poems. This
is certainly true of the ballads that make their appearance in all the novels, such things as the Ballad in *Headlong Hall,* beginning:

> O Mary, my sister, thy sorrow give o'er,
> I soon shall return, girl, and leave thee no more:
> But with children so fair, and a husband so kind
> I shall feel less regret when I leave thee behind.

or that of *Robin Hood and the Two Grey Friars* in *Maid
Marian*:

> Bold Robin has robed him in ghostly attire,
> And forth he is gone like a holy friar,
>   Singing, hey down, ho down, down, derry down:
> And of two grey friars he soon was aware.
> Regaling themselves with dainty fare,
>   All on the fallen leaves so brown.

Maid Marian especially is full of admirable words for
music, lyrics written with great gusto and with a fine
lilt, like this duet between Matilda and the Friar:

> Then follow, oh follow! the hounds do cry:
> The red sun flames in the eastern sky:
>   The stag bounds over the hollow.
> He that lingers in spirit, or loiters in hall,
> Shall see us no more till the evening fall,
> And no voice but the echo shall answer his call:
>   Then follow, oh follow, follow:
>   Follow, oh follow, follow!

> Though I be now a grey, grey friar,
>   Yet I was once a hale young knight:
> The cry of my dogs was the only choir
>   In which my spirit did take delight.
>
> Little I recked of matin bell,
>   But drowned its toll with my clanging horn
> And the only beads I loved to tell
>   Were the beads of dew on the spangled thorn.

The little sentimental songs, of which every one of the
novels can show a specimen or two, are of no importance, and we should require the music and the charming
voices of the young ladies who are supposed to sing them,
before we could be moved by their pale knights and lost
loves beyond the sea. We cannot, however, pass over
the song by Mr. Cypress in *Nightmare Abbey,* which is
a perfect *pastiche* (it cannot be called a parody) of the
Byronic style:

> There is a fever of the spirit,
>   The brand of Cain's unresting doom,
> Which in the lone dark souls that bear it
>   Glows like the lamp in Tullia's tomb.
> Unlike the lamp, its subtle fire
>   Burns, blasts, consumes its cell, the heart.
> Till, one by one, hope, joy, desire,
>   Like dreams of shadowy smoke depart. . . .

There is nothing to be compared with this in the rough-
and-ready attempts at parody to be found in *Sir Proteus*
and the *Paper Money Lyrics,* in both of which Peacock
has lost his wit with his geniality and is discovered
charging down his men rather than neatly pinking them.
More famous, and the supreme examples of Peacock's
lyrical wit in a sardonic vein, is the *War Song of Dinas
Vawr* from *The Misfortunes of Elphin,* which will be
found, quoted in full, in the pages devoted to that tale
in the next chapter but one. There are two other songs
from these novels equally well known, though the

one that has received more praise is not really the
better poem. This is *Love and Age,* from *Gryll
Grange,* in which Peacock captures with a light
hand a familiar experience, amusing in old age, with
mingled humour and pathos, over a long-lost love
affair:

> I played with you 'mid cowslips blowing,
>   When I was six and you were four;
> When garlands weaving, flower-balls throwing,
>   Were pleasures soon to please no more.
> Through groves and meads, o'er grass and heather,
>   With little playmates, to and fro,
> We wandered hand in hand together;
>   But that was sixty years ago. . . .

and so on, down the years, through love, estrangement,
full lives lived apart, children and grandchildren growing
up, until at last we come to the end:

> But though first love's impassioned blindness
>   Has passed away in colder light,
> I still have thought of you with kindness,
>   And shall do, till our last good-night.
> The ever-rolling silent hours
>   Will bring a time we shall not know,
> When our young days of gathering flowers
>   Will be an hundred years ago.

It has all the charm of a wise and kind and serene old
age, of which, indeed, it is the expression. More charming still, however, with a delicate loveliness that Peacock
never achieved elsewhere, is the earlier song from *Crotchet
Castle*:

> In the days of old,
> Lovers felt true passion,
> Deeming years of sorrow
> By a smile repaid.
> Now the charms of gold,
> Spells of pride and fashion,
> Bid them say good-morrow
> To the best-loved maid.

> Through the forests wild,
> O'er the mountains lonely,
> They were never weary
> Honour to pursue:
> If the damsel smiled
> Once in seven years only,
> All their wanderings dreary
> Ample guerdon knew.
>
> Now one day's caprice
> Weighs down years of smiling,
> Youthful hearts are rovers,
> Love is bought and sold:
> Fortune's gifts may cease,
> Love is less beguiling;
> Wiser were the lovers,
> In the days of old.

With its dainty and delicate measure, its fine frugality, its tender cadences, this lyric has all the antique grace and loveliness of an old-world dance, a saraband or pavan, played softly and exquisitely on the strings. It is the finest example of Peacock's sophisticated manner, of the occasional poet, turning aside from prose when he finds himself haunted by a little tune.

But love is not all: Bacchus has his rites, and it is not to be thought that in novels in which so many bottles are buzzed these rites will not be celebrated in song. There remain, then, the drinking-songs, a species of verse that would cut a very poor figure in modern English Literature if it were not for Peacock. The drinking-song demands a mingling of lilt, wit and gusto, and Peacock has all three. He makes a fair beginning in *Headlong Hall* with—

> In his last binn Sir Peter lies,
>   Who knew not what it was to frown:
> Death took him mellow, by surprise,
>   And in his cellar stopped him down.

and the rousing glee—

A heeltap! a heeltap! I never could bear it!

Melincourt has nothing to show in this vein except the lay of the three ghostly friars who have become merry ghosts and can cry—

> Let the ocean be Port, and we'll think it good sport
> To be laid in that Red Sea.

The brisk circulation of the bottle in *Nightmare Abbey* produces the famous *Seamen Three,* a truly Illyrian catch that would draw three souls out of one weaver:

> Seamen three! What men be ye?
> Gotham's three wise men we be.
> Whither in your bowl so free?
> To rake the moon from out the sea.
> The bowl goes trim. The moon doth shine.
> And our ballast is old wine;
> And your ballast is old wine.
>
> Who art thou, so fast adrift?
> I am he they call Old Care.
> Here on board we will thee lift.
> No: I may not enter there.
> Wherefore so? 'Tis Jove's decree,
> In a bowl Care may not be;
> In a bowl Care may not be.
>
> Fear ye not the waves that roll?
> No: in charmed bowl we swim.
> What the charm that floats the bowl?
> Water may not pass the brim.
> The bowl goes trim. The moon doth shine.
> And our ballast is old wine;
> And your ballast is old wine.

There is a fine suggestion of poetry happy in its cups about these verses, which are at once solemn and hilarious in a manner not unfamiliar to convivial circles. Not so well known but equally good, perhaps even better, is Mr. Trillo's song in *Crotchet Castle,* the last of Peacock's drinking-songs:

If I drink water while this doth last,
  May I never again drink wine:
For how can a man, in his life of a span,
  Do anything better than dine?
We'll dine and drink, and say if we think
  That anything better can be;
And when we have dined, wish all mankind
  May dine as well as we.

And though a good wish will fill no dish,
  And brim no cup with sack,
Yet thoughts will spring, as the glasses ring,
  To illumine our studious track.
On the brilliant dreams of our hopeful schemes
  The light of the flask shall shine;
And we'll sit all day, but we'll find the way
  To drench the world with wine.

This is as good as a bumper of the old Madeira it
celebrates.

So much for Peacock's achievement in verse. One
small volume will contain it all, and even in that volume
there will be a great deal that his most admiring reader
would gladly omit. Lacking passion, fertility, a strong
imagination, he is essentially a prose writer who happens
to be also an occasional poet. He did not find himself
until he turned to prose and only went back to verse
from time to time when he found himself commanded
by a genuine lyrical impulse. But his best verse is good
enough to stand on its own merits and has not come
down to us clinging to the coat-tails of his prose work.
Indeed, his best-known lyrics, such things as *The Grave
of Love, Seamen Three, The War Song of Dinas Vawr,
Youth and Age,* have had a far wider audience than the
tales from which three out of the four poems mentioned
have been taken, and thousands of readers who know their
anthologies of English Poetry are acquainted with Peacock the poet though not with Peacock the novelist. Had

the novels never survived their own age, Peacock would still have had a secure little place as the author of certain songs, graceful, tender, witty, hilarious, that will not be forgotten for many a year. In addition, there is his *Rhododaphne,* which wants the highest and rarest qualities of poetry, the sustained flight of the imagination, but to which some lovers of narrative verse will always want to return because of its shapeliness and bloom, its innumerable bright pictures of that antique world its author loved. The poet in Peacock cannot compare, in force and originality, with the prose humorist, but if we think of him as the occasional lyrical poet, not flashing into pure poetry, always a little deliberate, sophisticated, yet contriving to celebrate most happily uproarious goodfellowship or to express most exquisitely the familiar emotion of tender regret, we shall agree that the novelist has no reason to feel ashamed of his companion, the poet, who keeps pace with him down the years.

CHAPTER VI

HIS FICTION: THE NOVELS OF TALK

SOME description of Peacock's novels has already been given in the chapters recording his life. It will be remembered that two of his stories stand apart from the rest. These are the two "romances", *Maid Marian* and *The Misfortunes of Elphin,* which cannot be neglected—and critics have frequently dismissed them with a sentence or two—because they contain some of his most characteristic passages. Indeed, *The Misfortunes of Elphin,* as Mr. George Saintsbury has always pointed out, is composed of the Peacockian essence, so that it is astonishing to find critics professing an admiration for the man and yet passing by this sardonic little masterpiece of his with the most perfunctory salute. But as Peacock's fiction naturally falls into two tiny groups, we will begin with the larger, consisting of the five novels of opinion or talk. These are *Headlong Hall* (1816), *Melincourt* (1817), *Nightmare Abbey* (1818), *Crotchet Castle* (1831), and *Gryll Grange* (1861). In describing them as they appeared in the chronicle of their author's life, we have already noted certain differences between them. Thus, *Headlong Hall,* very short and with hardly any action, is the most generalised and abstract of them; *Melincourt,* the

longest, has more movement and suggests a definite
point of view, its satire being chiefly directed against
reactionary opinions, and is at once the most wildly
farcical and the most serious, containing some of the
maddest and the dullest chapters that Peacock ever
wrote; *Nightmare Abbey* satirises ultra-romantic gloom
and, with its neat little plot, has a greater resemblance
than any of the others to a stage comedy; *Crotchet
Castle,* the best of them, returns to a more detached point
of view and to the manner of *Headlong Hall,* but is less
farcical and abstract, is more human, diversified and
subtle; and *Gryll Grange,* the longest after *Melincourt,*
is the mildest and most urbane and comes nearest to
being a volume of learned table-talk. These are some
of the more obvious differences that obtrude themselves
when we are considering Peacock by himself. They fade
into insignificance, however, when we see his novels
against the background of fiction in general, which
throws into high relief their common likeness and their
originality. The fact that there may be individual differences between them is obliterated by the fact that one
and all are so unlike any other novels we have ever
known.

If we examine the earliest of them, *Headlong Hall,*
certain influences will suggest themselves, but they will
not take us very far. There can be no doubt that
Peacock had studied the eighteenth-century French *contes,*
in which characters frequently embody opinions and
discussion takes the place of action. Mr. Saintsbury
has pointed out that Miss Cranium, who is called
"the beautiful Cephalis", must have reminded Peacock
of *la belle Cephalide* in Marmontel's *Marriage samnites,
anecdote ancienne.* Mr. Carl van Doren has justly

observed that "the term philosopher, as applied to Mr. Escot, Mr. Foster, and Mr. Jenkinson, is a direct translation of *philosophe* as used in French revolutionary fiction"; though use of the term in this wider sense was not unknown in England. He also suggests that the Reverend Dr. Gaster, the first and worst of Peacock's parsons, "owes his existence less to the amenities of English theological controversy than to the sorry rôle played by the ecclesiastic in French satirical literature from the medieval fabliaux to the romances of the Revolution". But this is to have too keen a nose for influences: a young man, hostile to the Church, had no need in Regency England to import guzzling and ignorant clericals from continental literature. What Peacock did import was a certain manner of narration, in which the author only obtrudes himself in order to make some brief witty comment, the descriptive passages being polished and elegant, and the dialogue, existing in its own right, at once leisurely and pointed. This manner can be discovered in eighteenth-century French literature, from Anthony Hamilton onwards, and Peacock has it, though with some marked individual differences. There are, too, particularly in *Headlong Hall,* suggestions of the English eighteenth century. Thus, as one critic has pointed out, Peacock has caught Fielding's trick of describing some piece of horseplay and buffoonery not only quite gravely but also in a slightly heightened manner, as if it were an event in an epic. His occasional stately little set pieces of description, too, though rather warmer in tone and more concrete and exact, less generalised, frequently remind us of the earlier century. Moreover, as Mr. van Doren reminds us, "such novels as George Walker's very clever, though 'forgotten *Vagabond* (1799), and Isaac Disraeli's *Vaurien* (1797) and *Flim-Flams* (1805), had earlier shown almost the same influence (that of the French *contes*) in the embodiment of opinion in fiction, and they, too, had satirised living Englishmen." But in this matter of embodied opinions, greater influences than any yet mentioned were at work, for it was Peacock's belief, mentioned in his article for the *London Review* on *French Comic Romances,* that all the really great writers of comic fiction, such favourites of his as Aristophanes, Petronius, Rabelais, Voltaire, had always put opinion before character in their work, and had dealt with ideas rather than with human beings. And these writers undoubtedly provided Peacock with such models as he required, influencing him in a hundred different ways.

He may have borrowed a few ingredients, but the mixture is entirely his own. Perhaps the shortest way of describing these novels is to say that their action is talk. As Raleigh has remarked:

Talk gives the structure of his books. They are a world of talk. "It's all very fine talking," people say, "but is it practical?" In Peacock the standard is reversed. "It's all very practical, but is it fine talking?"

All his characters that are of any importance exist in order to talk. Once Peacock has brought them into his country house and set the wine in front of them, he retires as a narrator, merely letting us know who is speaking by putting a name above the speech, like a dramatist. The moments when the talk is in full flood are the real crises of these novels, the action of which exists either to bring about these moments or as a droll or sardonic commentary upon them. When we think

about these novels we do not remember what was
done but what was said, and on reading them again
we are generally surprised to find that they offer us
even some semblance of a plot. In the earlier novels,
particularly *Headlong Hall,* not only is Peacock at no
pains to conciliate the ordinary novel-reading public
but in places he is deliberately flying in its face. This
is his intellectual mischievousness. He will laugh at
novels while apparently writing one. Thus, he begins
Headlong Hall by indicating four travellers in the
Holyhead mail coach. They begin to talk about the
weather, and "the ice being thus broken, the colloquy
rambled to other topics, in the course of which it
appeared, to the surprise of every one, that all four,
though perfect strangers to each other, were actually
bound to the same point, namely Headlong Hall. . . ."
All these four gentlemen are provided with names
whose convenient etymology is explained by the in-
genious author in footnotes. The story might be said
to have a conventional plot, for it has an ardent young
man in love with a beautiful girl, whose father he saves
from drowning, and the father, in the best tradition,
refuses his consent and brings forward a richer suitor,
and is not won over until the very end of the story.
On this data the story is the conventional romance of
the time. But when most of the events connected
with this plot, such as the rescue of the father, are
described very briefly and drolly; when all the personages concerned always dismiss their own affairs to talk
about things in general; when the father is a Mr.
Cranium, the phrenologist, and is won over by being
presented with the skull of Cadwallader; when the
reader is coolly informed that the rejected suitor, on

being condoled with by the father, "begged him not
to distress himself on the subject, observing, that the
monotonous system of female education brought every
individual of the sex to so remarkable an approxima-
tion of similarity, that no wise man would suffer himself to be annoyed by a loss so easily repaired"; it
becomes obvious that whatever the author is doing, he
is certainly not plotting in the conventional manner.
After being tricked in this fashion, the ordinary novel-
reader retires in disgust from the study of Peacock, not
being like Mr. Panscope above who would not suffer
himself to be annoyed by a loss so easily repaired. And
if anything is needed to confirm that reader's suspicion
that the author is laughing at him, it is probably
supplied by the end of the story, when characters are
paired off at an astonishing rate. "Here," says the
Squire to Mr. Escot, "are three couple of us going to
throw off together, with the Reverend Doctor Gaster
for whipper-in: now, I think you cannot do better than
make the fourth with Miss Cephalis." This is indeed
Headlong Hall.

This deliberate flouting of the conventionalities of
fiction is never entirely absent from any of Peacock's
novels, but there is less and less of it as we move forward.
Indeed, before he has done, he commits himself to
a little half-serious plotting. The affairs of Captain
Fitzchrome and Lady Clarinda, of Mr. Chainmail and
Miss Susannah Touchandgo, in *Crotchet Castle,* of
Mr. Falconer and Miss Gryll, of Lord Curryfin and
Miss Niphet, in *Gryll Grange,* are all handled with a
certain seriousness, romantic zest, in spite of their droll
setting. Peacock, who, as we have already seen, always
remained something of a romantic at heart, really enjoyed

these passages of young and triumphant love, enjoyed
them, we suspect, more than he would have cared to
admit. In the earlier *Nightmare Abbey* there is none
of this half-serious romantic interest, but in its place
there is almost sufficient action, revolving about Scythrop's
simultaneous love affairs, but augmented by a certain
amount of comic by-play, to make the novel entertaining to readers who may not appreciate to the full its
capital talk. In *Melincourt,* however, Peacock undoubtedly presented the ordinary novel-reader with a choke-
pear. Yet it is well to remember that Mr. Forester
and his Anthelia, that excessively solemn, long-winded
and priggish pair of lovers, who seem to us to put
such obstacles in the way of any reader, can be matched
in a good deal of the conventional fiction of the time.
Most of the action of the novel, however, has for its
protagonist the civilised orang-outang, known as Sir Oran
Haut-ton, a character not to be matched in the fiction
of any time. Sir Oran does exactly what the hero of
conventional romance always does: he is always on
hand to rescue the heroine from mountain torrents and
kidnappers; and he may be said to be the first of our
strong silent heroes. This is one of Peacock's most
impudent strokes. For the rest, the most spirited chapters in *Melincourt* are those that describe the election,
a piece of glorious Aristophanic burlesque that is worlds
away from either the romance or realism of ordinary
fiction.

Let us admit, then, that the personages in these
novels do little but talk and that most of them—the
Milestones and Sir Simon Steeltraps and Henbanes
and Feathernests—are not creatures of this world but
simply so many personified ideas or interests. Does

this mean that *Headlong Hall* and the rest cannot really be considered novels at all? Are they best approached as so many comic dialogues? So some critics would seem to think, and one of them has described the Peacock novel as "a Platonic dialogue as Aristophanes might have caricatured it". This is an excellent description so long as we are allowed to assume that Aristophanes (who was certainly Peacock's greatest master) would have turned his dialogue into what we now call fiction. Otherwise it is misleading. Peacock's critics have been so anxious to point out that he did not write conventional fiction that they have frequently driven him away from the novel altogether. This, however, is a mistake because Peacock is, in his own queer way, a novelist, and his five tales of talk are just as far removed from philosophical dialogues and the like as they are from ordinary realistic fiction. They occupy a position—perhaps a unique position— between the two. It is one of the secrets of their appeal, this curious intermediate character of theirs, which makes them less concrete and documented than novels proper and yet far less abstract than such things as dialogues and allegories. Indeed, they are far less abstract, are nearer the earth, than a great many of the old artificial comedies. If these novels of his do not give us fully human records, neither do they transport us entirely to some abstract region of ideas. Their action passes in a world, even though it is a world at some remove from the one we know. It is easily recognised and quite unlike any other, so that we can say there is a Peacock world just as we say there is a Dickens world. Peacock, so unlike the great original novelists in almost every particular, at least resembles in this, that he has created a world of his own. And whatever difference there may be between *Headlong Hall* and *Gryll Grange, Melincourt* and *Crotchet Castle,* one and all take us to the same Peacock world.

It is of course a world of talk and talkers. Its personages are almost completely themselves when they are happily seated behind the decanters, each hammering away at his own theory. But there are also some women, fair and pleasant-spoken, and some romantic young lovers. Moreover, this world is provided with the scenery of romance. Consider this passage in the best of these novels, *Crotchet Castle* :

One day Mr. Chainmail traced upwards the course of a mountain-stream, to a spot where a small waterfall threw itself over a slab of perpendicular rock, which seemed to bar his farther progress. On a nearer view, he discovered a flight of steps, roughly hewn in the rock, on one side of the fall. Ascending these steps, he entered a narrow winding pass, between high and naked rocks, that afforded only space for a rough footpath carved on one side, at some height above the torrent.

The pass opened on a lake, from which the stream issued, and which lay like a dark mirror, set in a gigantic frame of mountain precipices. Fragments of rock lay scattered on the edge of the lake, some half-buried in the water: Mr. Chainmail scrambled some way over these fragments, till the base of a rock, sinking abruptly in the water, effectually barred his progress. He sat down on a large smooth stone; the faint murmur of the stream he had quitted, the occasional flapping of the wings of a heron, and at long intervals the solitary springing of a trout, were the only sounds that came to his ear. The sun shone brightly half-way down the opposite rocks, presenting, on their irregular faces, strong masses of light and shade. Suddenly he heard the dash of a paddle, and, turning his eyes, saw a solitary and beautiful girl gliding over the lake in a coracle. . . .

There is a passage that any romance might wear as a jewel. Nor would it be difficult to find companion passages, in which remote and beautiful places are described in a style that is vivid in spite of its obvious restraint. Even the comic debaters and crotcheteers are always provided with a charming or wild and picturesque background, far removed from bustle and noise and dirt. Thus the opening paragraph of *Crotchet Castle* takes us to an Arcadian countryside:

In one of these beautiful valleys, through which the Thames (not yet polluted by the tide, the scouring of cities, or even the minor defilement of the sandy streams of Surrey) rolls a clear flood through flowery meadows; under the shade of old beech woods, and the smooth mossy greensward of the chalk hills (which pour into it their tributary rivulets, are pure and pellucid as the fountain of Bandusium, or the wells of Scamander, by which the wives and daughters of the Trojans washed their splendid garments in the days of peace, before the coming of the Greeks); in one of those beautiful valleys, on a bold round-surfaced lawn, spotted with juniper, that opened itself in the bosom of an old wood, which rose with a steep, but not precipitous ascent, from the river to the summit of the hill, stood the castellated villa of a retired citizen.

And Headlong Hall is in the romantic Vale of Llanberis; Anthelia Melincourt has an old castle "in one of the wildest valleys in Westmoreland", where daily she sees "the misty mountain-top, the ash-fringed precipice, the gleaming cataract, the deep and shadowy glen, and the fantastic magnificence of the mountain clouds"; Nightmare Abbey very naturally has a more dismal setting, being situated somewhere between the sea and the Fens in Lincolnshire, but is equally picturesque and remote; and Gryll Grange, "on the borders of the New Forest, in the midst of a park which was a little forest in

itself, reaching nearly to the sea, and well-stocked with
deer", is clearly only a stone's throw from Arden itself.
This world of Peacock's, then, though it would seem
a world of intellectual comedy, is filled with Arcadian
countrysides and wildly romantic solitudes. The droll
debates and the bumpers of Madeira are set against a
background of quiet rivers and green shades, of the
gleaming cataract and the deep and shadowy glen. It
is the poet, the romantic, the idealist, in Peacock who
has touched in this background purely for his own good
pleasure.

If satire pure and simple—political, literary, social
satire—were his object, then it is curious that he should
have given us these idyllic or romantic settings instead
of taking us to London, that he should have assembled
all his characters in these remote places instead of
displaying them in their native haunt, the Town. It
is true that his house-party method, bringing all his
people under one roof and leaving them to entertain
one another, gives him a certain advantage, but this is
far outweighed by the advantage offered by the London
scene, which obviously is far richer in possibilities for
the satirist. But being something more than satirist,
being also a poet and humorist, Peacock preferred to
set his scene against these backgrounds because, we
repeat, their creation gave him pleasure. His imagination took refuge in these idyllic or romantic settings,
which represent one side of his mind just as the intellectual farce that is played there represents another.
The poet in him, who once wrote *The Philosophy of
Melancholy* and *Rhododaphne,* now find satisfaction in
idealising the scenes of the novels, and this he could
do quite safely, without any fear of being laughed at,

because he was already protected by the mockery in their action and characterisation. If the foreground in his fiction is mostly filled in with a caricature of what actually goes on in the world, its background gives us a sketch of what ought to go on in the world, of the author's ideal realm. There is something very piquant in the contrast, and piquancy, so welcome to sophisticated minds, has long been noted as one of Peacock's characteristics. If its presence has been noted, however, it has not been explained, simply because no explanation is possible so long as the satirist in him is allowed to hide completely the poet in him, so long as he is seen as a writer of comic dialogues only and not as a novelist, creating a world of his own in which his imagination can happily play. It is a very queer world, but it suited Peacock, whose novels were primarily a recreation, and, in spite of its obvious limitations, it is capable of providing rest and refreshment for any reader who brings to it a sense of humour.

It certainly provides rest and refreshment for its own creatures. For them it shows meat and drink They are only asked to bring out their pet theories, hold fast to them and remain entirely unconvinced by other people's arguments, slake their thirst and pass the bottle. However wildly different their views may be, they are all alike in their passion for talk and conviviality, in the gusto with which they give and take hospitality. Even the weirdest of them do not fail in these particulars: Mr. Mystic's life at Cimmerian Lodge is like a metaphysical nightmare, but nevertheless he puts before his guests a good dinner and "some superexcellent Madeira"; the gloom of Nightmare

Abbey does not prevent the rapid circulation of the bottle; and not one of the crotchets that are produced at the table in Crotchet Castle suggests any possible abstinence from the hock and champagne, the salmon and chicken and asparagus, to be found there. The worst reactionary and the wildest rebel of them all do not hesitate to fill a bumper or join in a chorus. All these persons, in spite of their completely different opinions, have a strong likeness to one another, and are clearly inhabitants of the same world, in which the really strange visitors, the monsters who never make their appearance, would be ascetics, skinflints, water-drinkers, people who like to go to bed early, people who refuse to talk. Here again there is idealisation, a droll kind of poetical heightening. If you are fond of ideas and debate and conviviality (as Peacock himself was and as most of his admirers are), then this fantastic world, in which every one seems to talk and dine for ever, in which all those things that interfere in base reality with argument over the bottle are stoutly kept at bay, is a paradise, even though a comic little paradise. That Peacock used this world of his for purposes of satire is a fact so obvious that it is not worth stressing, but the ideal elements in it, by means of which he achieves humour rather than satire, have been so generally over-looked that they must be thrown into relief at the outset.

The characters in these novels, most of whom have already been mentioned and partly examined in the biographical chapters, can be roughly divided into three classes; the crotcheteers in general, each with his domi-nating interest or theory; the caricatures of actual per-sons; and the more rounded and normal characters (including practically all the women), who range from mere faint sketches to complete individuals. All the novels, except *Gryll Grange,* are filled with crotcheteers. Some of them merely represent a dominating interest. Thus, Mr. Chromatic in *Headlong Hall* and Mr. Trillo in *Crotchet Castle* care about nothing (with the usual exceptions, applying to all these people, of hearty eating and drinking) but music. These personages are not amusing and are nothing but supers in the scene. On a slightly higher level are such characters as Mr. Cranium, with his phrenology, Mr. Asterias, who spends his life looking for a mermaid, Mr. Firedamp, who thinks that water is the evil principle, Mr. Henbane, with his passion for poisons and antidotes, and Mr. Philpot, who "thinks of nothing but the heads and tails of rivers". A little above these, because they play a larger part in their respective novels, are the three debaters from *Headlong Hall*: Mr. Foster, the perfectibilian; Mr. Escot, the deteriorationist; and Mr. Jenkinson, the statu-quo-ite; and such personages as those two medieval enthusiasts, Mr. Downderry and Mr. Chainmail. One of the best of these crotcheteers is Mr. Toobad in *Nightmare Abbey*. This character, as we have already seen, shares some of the grotesque opinions of Peacock's Bracknell friend, Newton, but in spite of that he can hardly be classed with the caricatures of actual persons. He believed that the supreme dominion of the world was given over for a while to the Evil Principle, hence his favourite quotation from Revelations: "Woe to the inhabiters of the earth and of the sea! For the devil is come among you, having great wrath, because he knoweth that he hath but a short time." Peacock makes this absurd person pop up, crying, "The devil is come among you", throughout the story, and is clever enough to make just sufficient use of him. There is something very droll in the way in which, triumphantly riding his hobby-horse, he contrives to find solid satisfaction in any disastrous event, which may injure him as a man but does at least flatter him as a theorist. But these crotcheteers, hanging the world on one interest or one opinion, are not very entertaining by themselves but only in the mass, when we see one after another following his nose and discovering in every statement of fact or event only a further proof of the truth of his opinion. As characters they are not important, but they are useful as a kind of chorus, hinting at wilder and wilder absurdities and antics of the human mind.

We now come to the second class of characters, made up of what we have called caricatures of actual persons. A list of those persons has already been given in the descriptions of the various novels as they appeared. But when we say, for example, that Mr. Feathernest and Mr. Mystic in *Melincourt* represent Southey and Coleridge, what do we mean? In exactly what sense can they be said to represent them? Only, it is clear, in a very restricted sense. Mr. Feathernest and Mr. Mystic are obviously not creatures of this world at all but are typical inhabitants of Peacock's own Cloud-Cuckoodom. And even there, where every person is inevitably strangely transformed, they are not really Southey and Coleridge. Peacock never disavowed deliberate caricature as, for example, Dickens did, yet Dickens's Harold Skimpole is far more like Leigh Hunt than any of Peacock's characters are like their victims. This is because Peacock did not represent Southey and

Coleridge in his two characters, but merely created two
fantastic creatures out of their opinions. With these
characters and the scenes in which they display themselves at length, he does what he maintained that all
the great comic writers did, he creates fiction out of
opinions. Although at times he may go too far, for
the most part he deals with his victims simply as public
persons and does not try to represent them in their
private life or make any reference to it. Thus,
Mr. Feathernest is not the actual Southey of Greta
Hall, Keswick, the unselfish, industrious, upright man
of letters, but simply some of Southey's more reactionary opinions endowed with Peacockian humanity.
His public life is, as it were, impudently dramatised by
the satirist. And in his methods Peacock frequently
adopts the system of his own amusing Mr. Sarcastic
in *Melincourt*. The passage in which Mr. Sarcastic
describes his system is well worth quoting for its own
sake.

Mr. Sarcastic
In my ordinary intercourse with the world I reduce
practice to theory; it is a habit, I believe, peculiar to myself,
and a source of inexhaustible amusement.

Sir Telegraph Paxarett
Fill and explain.

Mr. Sarcastic
Nothing, you well know, is so rare as the coincidence of
theory and practice. A man who "will go through fire and
water to serve a friend" in words, will not give five guineas
to save him from famine. A poet will write Odes to
Independence, and become the obsequious parasite of any
great man who will hire him. A burgess will hold up one
hand for purity of election, while the price of his own vote

is slily dropped into the other. I need not accumulate
instances.

MR. FORESTER

You would find it difficult, I fear, to adduce many to the
contrary.

MR. SARCASTIC

This, then, is my system. I ascertain the practice of
those I talk to, and present it to them as from myself, in
the shape of theory; the consequences of which is, that I
am universally stigmatised as a promulgator of rascally
doctrines. Thus I said to Sir Oliver Oilcake, "When I
get into Parliament I intend to make the sale of my vote as
notorious as the sun at noonday. I will have no rule of
right, but my own pocket. I will support every measure
of administration, even if they ruin half the nation for the
purpose of restoring the Great Lama, or of subjecting
twenty millions of people to be hanged, drawn, and quar-
tered at the pleasure of the man-milliner of Mahomet's
mother. I will have shiploads of turtle and rivers of
Madeira for myself, if I send the whole swinish multitude
to draff and husks." Sir Oliver flew into a rage, and swore
he would hold no further intercourse with a man who
maintained such infamous principles.

MR. HIPPY

Pleasant enough, to show a man his own picture, and
make him damn the ugly rascal.

MR. SARCASTIC

I said to Miss Pennylove, whom I knew to be *laying
herself out for a good match,* "When my daughter becomes
of marriageable age, I shall commission Christie to put her
up to auction, 'the highest bidder to be the buyer; and if
any dispute arise between two or more bidders, the lot to
be put up again and resold'". Miss Pennylove professed
herself utterly amazed and indignant that any man, and a
father especially, should imagine a scheme so outrageous
to the dignity and delicacy of the female mind.

THE HONOURABLE MRS. PINMONEY AND MISS DANARETTA
A most horrid idea certainly.

MR. SARCASTIC

The fact, my dear ladies, the fact; how stands the fact?
Miss Pennylove afterwards married a man old enough to
be her grandfather, for no other reason but because he was
rich; and broke the heart of a very worthy friend of mine,
to whom she had been previously engaged, who had no
fault but the folly of loving her, and was quite rich enough
for all the purposes of matrimonial happiness. How the
dignity and delicacy of such a person could have been
affected, if the preliminary negociation with her hobbling
Strephon had been conducted through the instrumentality
of honest Christie's hammer, I cannot possibly imagine.

MR. HIPPY

Nor I, I must say. All the difference is in the form,
and not in the fact. It is a pity that form does not come
into fashion; it would save a world of trouble.

MR. SARCASTIC

I irreparably offended the Reverend Doctor Vorax by
telling him, that having a nephew, whom I wished to shine
in the church, I was on the look-out for a luminous butler,
and a cook of solid capacity, under whose joint tuition he
might graduate. "Who knows," said I, "but he may immor-
talise himself at the University, by giving his name to a
pudding?"—I lost the acquaintance of Mrs. Cullender, by
saying to her, when she had told me a piece of gossip as
a very particular secret, that there was nothing so agreeable
to me as to be in possession of a secret, for I made a point
of telling it to all my acquaintance:

> Intrusted under solemn vows,
> Of Mum, and Silence, and the Rose,
> To be retailed again in whispers,
> For the easy credulous to disperse.

Mrs. Cullender left me in great wrath, protesting she
would never again throw away *her* confidence on so leaky
a vessel.

Peacock frequently makes use of this system with his
Feathernests and Vamps and Anyside Antijacks. Thus,
Southey came to change his early revolutionary views,
supported the Tory Government and was given a pen-
sion of £200 a year. Peacock promptly turns him into

a celebrated poet, Mr. Feathernest, to whom the Marquis
had recently given a place in exchange for his conscience.
It was thought by Mr. Feathernest's friends that he had
made a very good bargain. The poet had, in consequence,
burned his old *Odes to Truth and Liberty,* and had published a volume of Panegyrical Addresses "to all the
crowned heads in Europe", with the motto, "Whatever is
at court, is right".

Practice is promptly turned into theory: Mr. Feathernest is the frank advocate of remunerative apostasy.
"If there be any man who prefers a crust and water
to venison and sack, I am not of his mind," he cries;
and again—"Poets are verbal musicians, and, like other
musicians, they have a right to sing and play, where they
can be best paid for their music". A little later he
explains himself at length:

Truth and liberty, sir, are pretty words, very pretty
words—a few years ago they were the gods of the day—
they superseded in poetry the agency of mythology and
magic: they were the only passports into the poetical
market: I acted accordingly the part of a prudent man:
I took my station, became my own crier, and vociferated
Truth and Liberty, till the noise I made brought people
about me, to bid for me: and to the highest bidder I
knocked myself down, at less than I am worth certainly;
but when an article is not likely to keep, it is by no means
prudent to postpone the sale.

All this, of course, is grossly unfair; but then this cynical,
tippling personage bears not the slightest resemblance to

the real Southey, and Peacock is well aware of the fact. On the other hand, he disliked what he considered Southey's apostasy and his reactionary views, expressed with a humourless fervour in the *Quarterly,* and so made them the targets of his wit.

Because the *Quarterly* reviewers were always putting forward the insecurity of the Church as an excuse for steering clear of any reform, Peacock places them all into a room in Mainchance Villa and makes them answer or drown every progressive argument by crying in chorus: "The church is in danger! the church is in danger." In *Nightmare Abbey,* where the satire is more good-humoured, more subtle, and far more effective, Byron as Mr. Cypress is made to remark: "Sir, I have quarrelled with my wife; and a man who has quarrelled with his wife is absolved from all duty to his country," and is then compelled to paraphrase his elaborate lamentations from *Childe Harold* into pithy Peacockian prose and deliver them over the bottle, thereby making them sound very foolish. Shelley himself, as we have seen, is caricatured in this novel, and it is significant that he did not resent this appearance, a fact that throws further light on Peacock's methods and aims. For Shelley, who had watched his friend at work, knew very well that Peacock was not really putting him in the pillory, that Scythrop Glowry is a character composed out of one side of Shelley's mind and the common stuff of Peacockian humanity, which even in moments of despair, on the very verge of suicide, is always ready for a bottle of Madeira and a song. Scythrop's friend, Mr. Flosky, is another excellent example of Peacock's methods. Peacock admired Coleridge as a poet but could never resist the tempta-

✓ tion to caricature him, with the result that Coleridge makes an appearance in the first four novels and has more space devoted to him than any other contemporary. There are several reasons for this: his great position and wide influence made him a conspicuous figure; he was a rebel turned reactionary, like his friends Southey and Wordsworth; as a poet and dramatist, he was one of the chief representatives of the ultra-romantic "blue devil" school, which Peacock satirised in *Nightmare Abbey,* and as a philosopher, he professed those German metaphysical systems whose pretentiousness and uncouth jargon Peacock heartily disliked. In *Headlong Hall,* as Mr. Panscope, he can hardly be said to exist. The attempt in *Melincourt* is more ambitious, and we visit him, as Mr. Mystic, at Cimmerian Lodge. But here Peacock is too high fantastical to be effective, and we cannot help feeling that as yet he has not really done more than glance at Coleridge's prose work before attempting the caricature. In *Nightmare Abbey* he is more good-humoured, and is evidently working with a fuller knowledge of his man: the result is a piece of satire that is very amusing and impishly clever in its revelation of his victim's weaknesses. Following his usual method, Peacock makes Mr. Flosky explain himself:

. . . I pity the man who can see the connection of his own ideas. Still more do I pity him, the connection of whose ideas any other person can see. Sir, the great evil is, that there is too much commonplace light in our moral and political literature; and light is a great enemy to mystery, and mystery is a great friend to enthusiasm. Now the enthusiasm for abstract truth is an exceedingly fine thing, as long as the truth, which is the object of the enthusiasm, is so completely abstract as to be altogether out of the reach of the human faculties; and, in that sense,

I have myself an enthusiasm for truth, but in no other, for the pleasure of metaphysical investigation lies in the means, not in the end; and if the end could be found, the pleasure of the means would cease. . . .

And one of the best scenes in the book is that between Mr. Flosky and Marionetta, who wishes to know something about her cousin:

MARIONETTA

I must apologise for intruding on you, Mr. Flosky; but the interest which I—you—take in my cousin Scythrop——

MR. FLOSKY

Pardon me, Miss O'Carroll; I do not take any interest in any person or thing on the face of the earth; which sentiment, if you analyse it, you will find to be the quintessence of the most refined philanthropy.

MARIONETTA

I will take it for granted that it is so, Mr. Flosky; I am not conversant with metaphysical subtleties, but——

MR. FLOSKY

Subtleties! my dear Miss O'Carroll. I am sorry to find you participating in the vulgar error of the *reading public*, to whom an unusual collocation of words, involving a juxtaposition of antiperistatical ideas, immediately suggests the notion of hyperoxysophistical paradoxology.

MARIONETTA

Indeed, Mr. Flosky, it suggests no such notion to me. I have sought you for the purpose of obtaining information.

MR. FLOSKY (*shaking his head*)

No one ever sought me for such a purpose before.

MARIONETTA

I think, Mr. Flosky—that is, I believe—that is, I fancy—that is, I imagine——

Mr. Flosky

The τοῦτ᾽ ἐστί, the *id est,* the *cioè,* the *c'est-à-dire,* the *that is,* my dear Miss O'Carroll, is not applicable in this case— if you will permit me to take the liberty of saying so. Think is not synonymous with believe—for belief, in many most important particulars, results from the total absence, the absolute negation of thought, and is thereby the sane and orthodox condition of mind; and thought and belief are both essentially different from fancy, and fancy, again, is distinct from imagination. This distinction between fancy and imagination is one of the most abstruse and important points of metaphysics. I have written seven hundred pages of promise to elucidate it, which promise I shall keep as faithfully as the bank will its promise to pay.

Marionetta

I assure you, Mr. Flosky, I care no more about metaphysics than I do about the bank; and, if you will condescend to talk to a simple girl in intelligent terms——

Mr. Flosky

Say not condescend! Know you not that you talk to the most humble of men, to one who has buckled on the armour of sanctity, and clothed himself with humility as with a garment?

Marionetta

My cousin Scythrop has of late had an air of mystery about him, which gives me great uneasiness.

Mr. Flosky

That is strange: nothing is so becoming to a man as an air of mystery. Mystery is the very keystone of all that is beautiful in poetry, all that is sacred in faith, and all that is recondite in transcendental psychology. I am writing a ballad which is all mystery; it is "such stuff as dreams are made of", and is, indeed, stuff made of a dream; for, last night I fell asleep as usual over my book, and had a vision of pure reason. I composed five hundred lines in my sleep; so that, having had a dream of a ballad, I am now

officiating as my own Peter Quince, and making a ballad
of my dream, and it shall be called Bottom's Dream,
because it has no bottom.

And so on and so forth. Mr. Flosky is a glorious
absurdity, but he does contrive to burlesque the
Coleridge of *The Friend* and the *Aids to Reflection* with
wicked zest. Nor, however much we may happen to
admire Coleridge, can we deny that as the author of
such laboured, obscure, and over-solemn compositions,
he was fair game for any satirist. It is worth remembering, too, that if Peacock had gone to work with real
animosity towards the man himself, by making use of
facts concerning Coleridge's private life, facts that were
probably known to him, he could have produced a far
more damaging piece of satire. But here, as elsewhere,
he was only aiming at the public figure—the official
Coleridge, as it were, who was everybody's property—
and not at the private individual. This fact needs
stressing, and so does its companion fact, that Peacock's
method in these so-called caricatures was simply to take
a real person's theories, opinions, and so forth, and use
them as the basis of a character, which was completed
by the addition of the usual Peacockian traits. Mr.
Flosky and Mr. Feathernest and Mr. Cypress and the
rest really fare no worse than the others in the Peacock
world, for they have their seat at the table and their
share of the talk with all the other happy diners and
debaters.

The chief figures in the third class of characters are
the various hosts, the women, and the parsons. There
is little to be said about the hosts, Squire Headlong,
Mr. Glowry, Mr. Crotchet, Squire Gryll. Their part
is to issue invitations to all the eccentrics of their

acquaintance and then to see that the bottle is kept moving. Squire Headlong and Mr. Crotchet, we are told, had a passion for learned persons and disputation, and we try hard to believe that such indeed was the fact. Mr. Glowry has a point of view of his own, and Squire Gryll is not without learning and opinions, but they are little better than lay figures. The women begin by being lay figures, but gradually come to life with the development of Peacock's art. Thus the female characters in *Headlong Hall* are merely so many names and scraps of dialogue, but those in *Crotchet Castle* are lively and attractive individuals. Most critics have dismissed these women characters with a brief word, but Raleigh, in his notes on Peacock, has gone to the other extreme and given them the place of honour. Peacock's young ladies, he notes,

are real, perhaps because they are pleasant and sensible (which few of the men are), perhaps because the author takes fewer freedoms in the portraiture. It is difficult to say exactly how they make so pleasant an impression— probably by their freedom from consoriousness, and by the good will of the other characters towards them.

And he goes on to suggest that Meredith, "who learned more from Peacock than from any other writer", was especially indebted to his father-in-law for his characters of women. When we remember the proud position of Meredith's heroines, we can only regard this as a very great compliment indeed. Raleigh is too generous, however, though he is nearer the truth than those critics who dismiss all Peacock's women as so many ornamented sticks.

Anthelia Melincourt, who is more of a conventional heroine than any of the others, never contrives to catch

hold of our imagination at all. If she can be regarded
as a human being, then she must be considered an
incredibly stiff and priggish creature. Even when all
allowances have been made for the conventions of
dialogue in the old novel, it is difficult to feel any interest
or even believe in a young lady who always talks in
this way:

Both sexes, I am afraid, are too much influenced by the
spirit of mercenary calculation. The desire of competence
is prudence; but the desire of more than competence is
avarice: it is against the latter only that moral censure
should be directed: but I fear that in ninety-nine cases out
of a hundred in which the course of true love is thwarted
by considerations of fortune, it will be found that avarice
rather than prudence is to be considered as the cause. . . .

The thought of her marital dialogues with her equally
priggish and long-winded Mr. Forester makes us
shudder. Yet there is in Anthelia the faint outline of
a new and very attractive type of heroine, for she is
represented as being intelligent, cultivated, independent,
a distinct individuality, and yet not at all unfeminine.
Here perhaps is the protoplasm out of which Meredith,
bringing his own bright sunshine and strong air,
evolved his glorious women. There could have been
little development in Peacock's own comic world,
which is pre-eminently a masculine world, through
which his women lightly pass, smiling and singing.
In *Nightmare Abbey*, Celinda Toobad, who, as Stella,
becomes Scythrop's esoteric beloved, is merely a droll
sketch of feminine high-falutin', but her rival, Marionetta, pretty, vivacious, coquettish, has a fluttering life
of her own, and her scenes with her fantastic lover are
sufficiently convincing and are good comedy. Better

still, however, is Lady Clarinda, whom we may consider
the leading lady of *Crotchet Castle,* though its author
would probably prefer the claim of his Miss Touchandgo, a romantic figure in spite of her name. Lady
Clarinda is a delightful woman of the world and reminds
us of the great ladies of artificial comedy; she has their
cool sparkle, their good sense and wit and teasing airs.
In the chapter that describes the various eccentrics
who are gathered round the dining-table of Crotchet
Castle, Peacock uses Lady Clarinda as his mouthpiece,
and this change from direct to indirect description is
a considerable gain. Moreover, Lady Clarinda, at
once amused and detached and filled with fine feminine
common sense, is the ideal person to describe these
oddities. And Peacock has given her an individual
tone of voice, as it were, and it is just the right tone
of voice. How admirable is her teasing of her devoted
Captain!

Captain Fitzchrome

You always delighted in trying to provoke me; but I
cannot believe that you have not a heart.

Lady Clarinda

You do not like to believe that I have a heart, you mean.
You wish to think I have lost it, and you know to whom;
and when I tell you that it is still safe in my own keeping,
and that I do not mean to give it away, the unreasonable
creature grows angry.

Captain Fitzchrome

Angry! far from it: I am perfectly cool.

Lady Clarinda

Why you are pursing your brows, biting your lips, and
lifting up your foot as if you would stamp it into the earth.

I must say anger becomes you; you would make a charming Hotspur. Your every-day-dining-out face is rather insipid: but I assure you my heart is in danger when you are in the heroics. It is so rare, too, in these days of smooth manners, to see anything like natural expression in a man's face. There is one set form for every man's face in female society; a sort of serious comedy, walking gentleman's face: but the moment the creature falls in love, he begins to give himself airs, and plays off all the varieties of his physiognomy from the Master Slender to the Petruchio; and then he is actually very amusing.

There is genuine character in this raillery. But throughout Peacock contrives at last to blend character and satire, as in such passages as this:

LADY CLARINDA

Well, I will tell you a secret: I am writing a novel.

CAPTAIN FITZCHROME

A novel!

LADY CLARINDA

Yes, a novel. And I shall get a little finery by it: trinkets and fal-lals, which I cannot get from papa. You must know I have been reading several fashionable novels, the fashionable this, and the fashionable that; and I thought to myself, why I can do better than any of these myself. So I wrote a chapter or two, and sent them as a specimen to Mr. Puffall, the bookseller, telling him they were to be a part of the fashionable something or other, and he offered me, I will not say how much, to finish it in three volumes, and let him pay all the newspapers for recommending it as the work of a lady of quality, who had made very free with the characters of her acquaintance.

CAPTAIN FITZCHROME

Surely you have not done so?

LADY CLARINDA

Oh, no; I leave that to Mr. Eavesdrop. But Mr. Puffall made it a condition that I should let him say so.

These remarks express the character who utters them and also enable Peacock to make his satirical point. Incidentally, it will be found that he does it more neatly and effectively than Thackeray, who hunted the same quarry in such satirical papers as *The Fashionable Authoress*.

The best of all these general characters, however, is not Lady Clarinda but her companion in the same volume, the Rev. Dr. Folliott. We are told that Peacock described this character as his *amende honorable* to the Church of England, which had cut a very poor figure in his earlier novels in the persons of Dr. Gaster, of *Headlong Hall,* the Reverend Mr. Grovelgrub, in *Melincourt,* the Mr. Larynx of *Nightmare Abbey.* Whether all the members of that Church would care to accept Dr. Folliott as an adequate apology is not a question that Peacock discusses. There is nothing very spiritual about the Doctor, who would have remained much the same man if Christianity had never come into existence. But unlike his clerical predecessors, he is the very best of company. In the Peacock world of dining, wining, and debating, he is an ideal figure, for he dines and drinks and talks both learnedly and enthusiastically. If there is ever an Epicurean Church, he should be one of its saints. Here again, and to a higher degree, Peacock contrives to blend character and satire. Dr. Folliott is his creator's mouthpiece at every other moment, and his talk is a mine of satire. Nevertheless, there is nothing of the lay figure about him; we see him as a real person; he has an attitude of mind and a tone of voice of his own; and though Peacock put a great deal of himself into him, he is not to be taken for a mere mask, but is a genuine creation. He might be shortly described, however, as a projection and heightening of one side of Peacock's mind, the Tory, Greek-loving, Epicurean, anti-reform, unromantic side. This explains why he is portrayed with such gusto, but every reader must be warned against carrying the identification of author and character too far, a mistake made by many critics, who imagine they have been describing Peacock when in reality they have been describing Dr. Folliott. The romantic Peacock, with his idylls among the Welsh mountains and so forth, is worlds away from Dr. Folliott, and there are times when Peacock is laughing at his worthy Doctor's limitations and prejudices just as heartily as he laughs at those of his lesser figures.

Dr. Folliott is as crotchety as any of the other people at Crotchet Castle, but having more gusto and wit and pugnacity, he carries it off better than the others. He is a scholar and an epicure and, being very comfortable himself, he wants everything to be left untouched so that he can enjoy his Greek and his dinner in peace. As old things are obviously the best, old books, old wine, old customs, it is therefore monstrous folly to want to chop and change. People who desire such changes, who come disturbing the peace, are either rascals, feathering their nests, or idiots, who have not the sense and taste to see that no real improvement is possible, that the golden age was in the past and that therefore all innovations are disastrous. This is the secret of his intense conservatism, and it is well to remember that Seithenyn in *The Misfortunes of Elphin,* with his absurd defence of his policy of leaving the crumbling embankment to look after itself, is only Dr. Folliott seen, as it were, from the reverse side. With a mind so constituted, and with humour, wit, learning, and polemical acuteness to aid him, Dr. Folliott is a dangerous if genial adversary. He has a lightning eye for the absurd pretensions of too complacent reformers and cranks in general, and as his company consists for the most part of such persons, he deals execution right and left. Peacock deliberately brings most of the cant of the age before him, and very little of it escapes. He reminds us of Dr. Johnson in his ready and sometimes unscrupulous repartee and in his ability, when such methods are obviously of no avail, to use other weapons, notably his bamboo, with which he lays out the footpads. But his manner and talk are all his own and have the Peacockian sparkle and salty tang.

He displays himself at once in his initial outburst:

"God bless my soul, sir!" exclaimed the Reverend Doctor Folliott, bursting, one fine May morning, into the breakfast-room at Crotchet Castle, "I am out of all patience with this march of mind. Here has my house been nearly burned down, by my cook taking it into her head to study hydrostatics, in a sixpenny tract, published by the Steam Intellect Society, and written by a learned friend who is for doing all the world's business as well as his own, and is equally well qualified to handle every branch of human knowledge. I have a great abomination of this learned friend; as author, lawyer, and politician, he is *triformis,* like Hecate: and in every one of his three forms he is *bifrons,* like Janus; the true Mr. Facing-both-Ways of Vanity Fair. My cook must read his rubbish in bed; and as might naturally be expected, she dropped suddenly fast asleep, overturned the candle, and set the curtains in a blaze. Luckily, the footman went into the room at the moment, in time to tear down the curtains and throw them into the chimney, and a pitcher of water on her nightcap extinguished her wick: she is a greasy subject, and would have burned like a short mould."

And in a few moments he is set going again, this time
by Mr. MacQuedy who, as an economist and a Scot,
is one of the Doctor's chief butts:

MR. MacQUEDY

Then, sir, I presume you set no value on the right
principles of rent, profit, wages, and currency?

THE REV. DR. FOLLIOTT

My principles, sir, in these things are, to take as much
as I can get, and to pay no more than I can help. These
are every man's principles, whether they be the right
principles or no. There, sir, is political economy in a
nutshell.

MR. MacQUEDY

The principles, sir, which regulate production and con-
sumption, are independent of the will of any individual as
to giving or taking, and do not lie in a nutshell by any means.

THE REV. DR. FOLLIOTT

Sir, I will thank you for a leg of that capon.

LORD BOSSNOWL

But, sir, by-the-bye, how came your footman to be going
into your cook's room? It was very providential to be
sure, but——

THE REV. DR. FOLLIOTT

Sir, as good came of it, I shut my eyes, and asked no
questions. I suppose he was going to study hydrostatics,
and he found himself under the necessity of practising
hydraulics.

MR. FIREDAMP

Sir, you seem to make very light of science.

THE REV. DR. FOLLIOTT

Yes, sir, such science as the learned friend deals in:
everything for everybody, science for all, schools for all,
rhetoric for all, law for all, physic for all, words for all, and

sense for none. I say, sir, law for lawyers, and cookery for cooks: and I wish the learned friend, for all his life, a cook that will pass her time in studying his works; then every dinner he sits down to at home, he will sit on the stool of repentance.

The whole scene that follows, in which the Scots as the New Athenians, Kant (who "wants the two great requisites of head and tail"), and other subjects are discussed and promptly dismissed, is filled with the ripest Peacockian humour. Among other things, there is a droll little passage between the Doctor and Lord Bossnowl, after they have both been invited to go on a cruise up the Thames and Severn.

LORD BOSSNOWL
I hope, if I am to be of the party, our ship is not to be the ship of fools: He! He!

THE REV. DR. FOLLIOTT
If you are one of the party, sir, it most assuredly will not: Ha! Ha!

LORD BOSSNOWL
Pray, sir, what do you mean by Ha! Ha!

THE REV. DR. FOLLIOTT
Precisely, sir, what you mean by He! He!

Better still is his little conversation with the stranger (Captain Fitzchrome) that very same morning. It is too long to quote in full. But how blandly, in the little exchanges that follow, the Doctor takes the wind out of the sails of his crudely satirical interlocutor!

THE STRANGER
I beg your pardon, sir: do I understand this place to be your property?

THE REV. DR. FOLLIOTT

It is not mine, sir: the more is the pity; yet it is so far well, that the owner is my good friend, and a highly respectable gentleman.

THE STRANGER

Good and respectable, sir, I take it, mean rich?

THE REV. DR. FOLLIOTT

That is their meaning, sir.

And, a moment later:

THE STRANGER

Young Mr. Crotchet, sir, has been, like his father, the architect of his own fortune, has he not? An illustrious example of the reward of honesty and industry?

THE REV. DR. FOLLIOTT

As to honesty, sir, he made his fortune in the city of London; and if that commodity be of any value there, you will find it in the price current. I believe it is below par, like the shares of young Crotchet's fifty companies. . . .

It is he who dominates the situation that evening when, after dinner, the younger Crotchet announces that he will put into the hands of the company present a large sum of money for the purpose of regenerating society. This is enough for all the theorists round the table; and, after a lively skirmish between Dr. Folliott and Mr. MacQuedy, it goes on—

MR. MACQUEDY

Very true, sir (*reproducing his scroll*). "In the infancy of society——"

MR. TOOGOOD

The reverend gentleman has hit the nail on the head. It is the distribution that must be looked to: it is the paterfamilias that is wanting in the state. Now here I have provided him. (*Reproducing his diagram.*)

Mr. Trillo

Apply the money, sir, to building and endowing an opera
house, where the ancient altar of Bacchus may flourish,
and justice may be done to sublime compositions. (*Producing a part of a manuscript opera.*)

Mr. Skionar

No, sir, build *sacella* for transcendental oracles to teach
the world how to see through a glass darkly. (*Producing
a scroll.*)

Mr. Trillo

See through an opera-glass brightly.

The Rev. Dr. Folliott

See through a wine-glass, full of claret: then you see
both darkly and brightly. But, gentlemen, if you are all in
the humour for reading papers, I will read you the first
half of my next Sunday's sermon. (*Producing a paper.*)

Omnes

No sermon! No sermon!

The Rev. Dr. Folliott

Then I move that our respective papers be committed
to our respective pockets.

In the end the only agreement that can be reached is
that the fund should be spent on deliberative dinners,
which very Peacockian conclusion has the full approval
of Dr. Folliott. We cannot follow this ripe reverend
gentleman any further, and his wit and humour and
scholarship and vast array of prejudices must be sought
for in the droll little masterpiece that contains him.
It is sufficient to add that in him the Peacock world
reaches its fullest individual life. The far more celebrated Dr. Middleton of *The Egoist* is only Dr. Folliott

over again, with some gain in subtlety but an equal loss
in raciness, geniality, drollery.

It should hardly be necessary now—for even those
readers who do not know their Peacock must have made
the discovery for themselves—to indicate where his
strength lies in these novels. They consist for the
most part of talk, and it will have been noticed that
when the talk is in full swing, the narrator withdraws
himself altogether, being content, like a dramatist, to
let the dialogue carry him on. It is obvious that the
talk must have a special quality of its own, and indeed,
that the whole narratives must have some unusual
appeal to compensate us for their narrow scope and
lack of ordinary interest. This special quality, this
compensating appeal, is found, of course, in Peacock's
style. "I know not how to praise sufficiently the
lightness, chastity, and strength of the language of the
whole," wrote Shelley, of *Nightmare Abbey*. This
may be said of Peacock throughout his work, though
his style is seen at its best, having gained in ease and
piquancy, in *Crotchet Castle* and *The Misfortunes of
Elphin*. To the latter we will return in the next
chapter: our present concern is with *Crotchet Castle*
and its companions, the novels of talk. The secret of
Peacock's success in these odd productions is chiefly
to be found in the piquantly flavoured dialogue. His
manner, like that of all genuine ironists, is nearly always
grave and restrained. He does not try to be playful,
facetious. His writing always seems almost colourless
and stilted. Yet his style has a distinct flavour of its
own, and he is really just as personal a stylist as a Lamb
or a Carlyle. All his people, in spite of individual
differences, which are more marked in the later novels,

talk in the same way, like members of one closely united family. They all talk in crisp phrases, delicately balanced and full of antithesis, and with a precision that is at once admirable and droll. However wild their opinions and arguments may be, their actual statements of them are all given an epigrammatic brevity and ring. Thus the maddest of them is something of a stylist and a wit. But this very fact gives all their speeches, which usually put forward some ridiculous notion, a curious undercurrent of irony. They explain themselves, as it were, only too well: there is mockery in the very precision of their language and the crisp rhythm of their phrases. If, setting aside the obvious absurdities, you miss this constant undercurrent of irony, this faint mockery in the very neatness of the dialogue, this grave mischievousness in the style itself, a style like an old dry wine, you will probably fail to understand, as so many excellent persons have failed to understand, the enduring appeal of Peacock. The idea, sometimes put forward by his critics, that he cannot be enjoyed by readers unacquainted with the notions and persons he satirised, is quite untrue, although a knowledge of his age undoubtedly heightens the comedy. What he certainly does demand, however, is both a sense of humour and a fine literary palate.

That this real strength is to be found in his style is proved by an examination of *Headlong Hall,* by no means the best of these novels. In *Headlong Hall* he is working very stiffly and making use of actual quotations, yet how deftly and drolly he contrives all the Mr. Milestone business, for the most part based on controversial volumes and articles in reviews. Here is

Milestone showing his plan for the improvement of Lord Littlebrain's park:

MR. MILESTONE

. . . Now observe the metamorphosis. Here is the same rock, cut into the shape of a giant. In one hand he holds a horn, through which that little fountain is thrown to a prodigious elevation. In the other is a ponderous stone, so exactly balanced as to be apparently ready to fall on the head of any person who may happen to be beneath: and there is Lord Littlebrain walking under it.

SQUIRE HEADLONG
Miraculous, by Mahomet!

MR. MILESTONE
This is the summit of a hill, covered, as you perceive, with wood, and with those mossy stones scattered at random under the trees.

MISS TENORINA
What a delightful spot to read in, on a summer's day! The air must be so pure, and the wind must sound so divinely in the tops of those old pines!

MR. MILESTONE
Bad taste, Miss Tenorina. Bad taste, I assure you. Here is the spot improved. The trees are cut down; the stones are cleared away: this is an octagonal pavilion, exactly on the centre of the summit: and there you see Lord Littlebrain, on the top of the pavilion, enjoying the prospect with a telescope.

SQUIRE HEADLONG
Glorious, egad!

MR. MILESTONE
Here is a rugged mountainous road, leading through impervious shades: the ass and the four goats characterise

a wild uncultured scene. Here, as you perceive, it is totally changed into a beautiful gravel-road, gracefully curving through a belt of limes: and there is Lord Littlebrain driving four-in-hand.

SQUIRE HEADLONG
Egregious, by Jupiter!

MR. MILESTONE
Here is Littlebrain Castle, a Gothic, moss-grown structure, half bosomed in trees. Near the casement of that turret is an owl peeping from the ivy.

SQUIRE HEADLONG
And devilish wise he looks.

MR. MILESTONE
Here is the new house, without a tree near it, standing in the midst of an undulating lawn: a white, polished, angular building, reflected to a nicety in this waveless lake: and there you see Lord Littlebrain looking out of the window.

SQUIRE HEADLONG
And devilish wise he looks too. You shall cut me a giant before you go.

Yet even Mr. Milestone, whose every phrase in the passage above has a curious silliness about it, has his moment:

"Sir," said Mr. Milestone, "you will nave the goodness to make a distinction between the picturesque and the beautiful."
"Will I?" said Sir Patrick, "och! but I won't. For what is beautiful? That what pleases the eye. And what pleases the eye? Tints variously broken and blended. Now, tints variously broken and blended constitute the picturesque."

"Allow me," said Mr. Gall. "I distinguish the picturesque and the beautiful, and I add to them, in the laying out of grounds, a third and distinct character, which I call *unexpectedness.*"

"Pray, sir," said Mr. Milestone, "by what name do you distinguish this character, when a person walks round the grounds for the second time?"

Mr. Gall bit his lips, and inwardly vowed to revenge himself on Milestone, by cutting up his next publication.

Peacock has taken all this, as his footnote shows, from the controversy between Knight and the *Edinburgh Review,* yet his style, so neat and crisp and curiously salted with humour, makes it all his own, a typical Peacock passage. Whatever he transported into his own world, whatever comes to have expression through the medium of his style, is immediately saturated with this individual humour of his, at once so genial and dry, a curious mingling of mockery and good fellowship. And the style of his dialogue is so contrived that there seem to be undertones and overtones of irony and humour in these speeches: there is even laughter between the lines.

CHAPTER VII

HIS FICTION: THE TWO TALES

PEACOCK'S two remaining pieces of fiction, *Maid Marian*
and *The Misfortunes of Elphin,* would seem at first
sight to be far less original or wilfully eccentric compositions than the five novels of talk. Yet on examination they prove to be no nearer conventional historical
romance than the others are to conventional novels of
manners. They are equally whimsical productions, quite
unlike anything else in English literature. *Maid Marian,*
the earlier, is the less important. Some account of the
sources of the plot and of the general character of the
tale has already been given in Chapter III. At the
opening of the narrative, Robert Fitz-Ooth, Earl of
Locksley and Huntingdon, is being married to the
beautiful Matilda Fitzwater, daughter of the Baron of
Arlingford, at Rubygill Abbey. But before the cere-
mony can be concluded, the chapel is invaded by troops,
whose leader declares Fitz-Ooth an outlaw. The Earl
and his men fight their way out and finally take to the
greenwood, becoming Robin Hood and his band of outlaws. Matilda returns home, is confined to the castle
by her father, but escapes to the forest and joins her
lover there. She is accompanied by her confessor, Friar
Michael, who soon calls himself Friar Tuck, just as

his mistress calls herself Maid Marian. Prince John himself, having fallen in love with the lady and receiving no encouragement, besieges her father's castle. The Prince is defeated, but the castle is burnt down, and the old Baron himself joins the outlaws. The rest of the narrative, which is very episodic, gives us some of the traditional adventures of Robin Hood and his men. In the end, a strange knight is entertained by the outlaws, is discovered to be King Richard, and restores the various titles and estates of his companions. We are then told that after Richard's death, Robin and his lady and their friar returned to their greenwood sovereignty "and in merry Sherwood they long lived together, the lady still retaining her former name of Maid Marian, though the appellation was then as much a misnomer as that of Little John".

The action of the story is a mixture of romantic adventure and farce. Its setting is purely romantic, the Sherwood of these foresters being another Arden. There is more than a hint of Peacock's genuine and enduring passion for the open air and the woods in this idyllic background. It was probably this, more than anything else, that led him to the Robin Hood theme. He has no concern with the medieval scene, makes no attempt to paint the manners of the time, and it is more likely than not that the numerous anachronisms in the tale are quite deliberate. But the romantic element in him welcomed an idealised forest life. This journey back into the past also presented the satirist in him, who very quickly took command, with new opportunities. He discovered the trick of satirising the present in terms of the past, and satirising the past in terms of the present. By re-telling these old heroic legends in his own fashion, he could laugh at the world anew. This he proceeds to do, most heartily. He sketches in the historical background in this manner:

The departure of King Richard from England was succeeded by the episcopal regency of the bishops of Ely and Durham. Longchamp, bishop of Ely, proceeded to show his sense of Christian fellowship by arresting his brother bishop, and despoiling him of his share in the government; and to set forth his humility and loving-kindness in a retinue of nobles and knights who consumed in one night's entertainment some five years' revenue of their entertainer, and in a guard of fifteen hundred foreign soldiers, whom he considered indispensable to the exercise of a vigour beyond the law in maintaining wholesome discipline over the refractory English. The ignorant impatience of the swinish multitude with these fruits of good living, brought forth by one of the meek who had inherited the earth, displayed itself in a general ferment, of which Prince John took advantage to make the experiment of getting possession of his brother's crown in his absence. He began by calling at Reading a council of barons, whose aspect induced the holy bishop to disguise himself (some say as an old woman, which, in the twelfth century, perhaps might have been a disguise for a bishop), and make his escape beyond sea. . . .

He frequently makes use of the position of Robin Hood in his Sherwood as an excuse for satirising political power, as in the address by Friar Tuck:

. . . Robin Hood is king of the forest both by dignity of birth and by virtue of his standing army: to say nothing of the free choice of his people, which he has indeed, but I pass it by as an illegitimate basis of power. He holds his dominion over the forest, and its horned multitude of citizen deer, and its swinish multitude or peasantry of wild boars, by right of conquest and force of arms. He levies contributions among them by the free consent of his archers, their virtual representatives. If they should find a voice to complain that we are "tyrants and usurpers to kill and cook them up in their assigned and native dwelling-place", we should most convincingly admonish them, with point of arrow, that they have nothing to do with our laws but to obey them. Is it not written that the fat ribs of the herd shall be fed upon by the mighty in the land? And have they not withal my blessing? my orthodox, canonical, and archiepiscopal blessing? Do I not give thanks for them when they are well roasted and smoking under my nose? What title had William of Normandy to England that Robin of Locksley has not to merry Sherwood? William fought for his claim. So does Robin. With whom, both? With any that would or will dispute it. William raised contributions. So does Robin. From whom, both? From all that they could or can make pay them. Why did they pay them to William? Why do any pay them to Robin? For the same reason to both: because they could not or cannot help it. They differ indeed, in this, that William took from the poor and gave to the rich, and Robin takes from the rich and gives to the poor: and therein is Robin illegitimate; though in all else he is true prince. . . .

and so on to the sermon's end. There are some further sarcasms in the same vein:

So Robin and Marian dwelt and reigned in the forest, ranging the glades and the greenwoods from the matins of the lark to the vespers of the nightingale, and administering natural justice according to Robin's ideas of rectifying the inequalities of human condition: raising genial dews from the bags of the rich and idle, and returning them in fertilising showers on the poor and industrious: an operation which more enlightened statesmen have happily reversed, to the unspeakable benefit of the community at large. . . .

It is the familiar Peacock manner, though it is not that manner at its best.

Indeed, Peacock is far from being at his best in this tale. The idea of using romantic narrative, or rather the raw material of romantic narrative, chiefly for a satirical purpose, and yet keeping a suggestion of romance, a touch of idealisation, throughout, is a very excellent one. Unfortunately, in this first tale Peacock has not been able to blend his widely different elements, and instead of achieving a rich genial irony, he alternates between high spirits and rather rough sarcasm. His narrative is far too disjointed to be attractive in itself, and his characters, with one notable exception, are of no great interest. The exception is Friar Michael or Friar Tuck as he comes to be called, who dominates the tale. This singing, laughing, roaring, joke-crack-ing, bottle-cracking, skull-cracking friar—as the Baron describes him—is the best of Peacock's characters after Dr. Folliott and Prince Seithenyn. He is clearly a near relation of the Friar John of the Funnels of Rabelais, but he is sufficiently original to claim an independent existence. He is a tall man of his hands and frequently does great execution with his staff, but his real business is to make witty remarks and break into snatches of song. As we have seen already, there is about this tale a curious suggestion of the comic opera into which it was afterwards actually transformed. The sharp exchanges of dialogue, the frequent songs and catches, the somewhat theatrical background, the bloodless and farcical combats that never seem more than play, all these help to suggest comic opera, and the friar, the dominating character, does nothing to destroy the resemblance. It is not that he is an unreal theatrical figure, but his talk and his songs turn the action of the tale into a mere play of shadows and the baronial hall or forest glades into so many back-cloths. Such scenes as that in the fourth chapter,

between Matilda, the Baron, and the friar, are frankly
operatic:

"Under favour, bold baron," said the friar; but the friar
was warm with canary, and in his singing vein; and he
could not go on in plain unmusical prose. He therefore sang
in a new tune,—

> Though I be now a grey, grey friar,
>   Yet I was once a hale young knight:
> The cry of my dogs was the only choir
>   In which my spirit did take delight.
>
> Little I recked of matin bell,
>   But drowned its toll with my clanging horn:
> And the only beads I loved to tell
>   Were the beads of dew on the spangled thorn.

The baron was going to storm, but the friar paused, and
Matilda sang in repetition,—

> Little I reck of the matin bell,
>   But drown its toll with my clanging horn:
> And the only beads I love to tell
>   Are the beads of dew on the spangled thorn.

And then she and the friar sang the four lines together,
and rang the changes upon them alternately.

> Little I reck of the matin bell,

sang the friar.

"A precious friar," said the baron.

> But drown its toll with my clanging horn,

sang Matilda.

"More shame for you," said the baron.

> And the only beads I love to tell
>   Are the beads of dew on the spangled thorn,

sang Matilda and the friar together.

"Penitent and confessor," said the baron: "a hopeful
pair truly."

The friar went on,—

> An archer keen I was withal,
>   As ever did lean on greenwood tree;
> And could make the fleetest roebuck fall,
>   A good three hundred yards from me.
> Though changeful time, with hand severe,
>   Has made me now these joys forego,
> Yet my heart bounds whene'er I hear
>   Yoicks! hark away! and tally ho!

Matilda chimed in as before.

"Are you mad?" said the baron. "Are you insane? Are you possessed? What do you mean? What in the devil's name do you both mean?"

> Yoicks! hark away! and tally ho!

roared the friar.

Such scenes would obviously be more successful on the stage than they are in cold print. But the songs into which the friar breaks at every other turn do not seem unnatural, his high spirits finding no relief in prose. He is the master of the ceremonies at these greenwood revels, and the whole tale is nothing more than a revel, a frolic among the leaves, a matching of wits and balladry over venison pasty and flagons of canary. And he it is who comes nearest to expressing what Peacock would ask us to believe was his creed: "But you are welcome to laugh if it so please you. None shall laugh in my company, though it be at my expense but I will have my share of the merriment. The world is a stage, and life is a farce, and he that laughs most has most profit of the performance. The worst thing is good enough to be laughed at, though it be good for nothing else; and the best thing, though it be good for something else, is good for nothing better."

In *The Misfortunes of Elphin,* as we have already noted, Peacock followed the same method he had employed in *Maid Marian,* taking hold of an extremely romantic narrative and treating it satirically. The satire, of course, is not directly aimed at the romance in hand but at things in general. The later story, however, is far more piquant if only because the material, from Celtic legend, is more wildly romantic, being very vague, very Celtic, very legendary, and the treatment of it is more closely sardonic, the easy high spirits of *Maid Marian* being replaced by very dry humour and smooth irony. Despite its brevity and the space occupied by verses, it is Peacock's most ambitious attempt at narrative. We know that he spent a great deal of time exploring the old Welsh legends and finally fusing together three of them to make one reasonably compact tale. The first legend was that of the inundation of the Great Plain of Gwaelod. This plain was protected by an enormous embankment, which had watch-towers along its length and a central castle where dwelt the Lord High Commissioner of Royal Embankment, Prince Seithenyn, who spent his time carousing with his staff and left his great sea-wall to look after itself. In Peacock's version, Prince Elphin, the son of King Gwythno of Caredigion, the kingdom in which the Plain of Gwaelod is situated, hears a mysterious warning voice and then receives a visit from one Teithrin, a subordinate of Seithenyn's who happens to be conscientious in his duties. Elphin is told by Teithrin that the embankment is in a state of ruinous decay. Together they visit Seithenyn in his castle to demand an explanation. That very night, during a storm, the high tide breaks down the embankment and the plain is submerged. Elphin and Teithrin, together with Seithenyn's daughter, Angharad, and one or two other persons, contrive to escape by walking along the top of the great wall to the high land. Afterwards Elphin marries Angharad and becomes king of the reduced Caredigion. We are now carried forward to the Taliesin legends. A sleeping child is found in a coracle in the salmon weir that Elphin has constructed. This child is adopted by Elphin and Angharad, and becomes the wonderful bard, Taliesin. He is in love with Elphin's daughter, Melanghel. The rest of the tale turns on the efforts of Taliesin to free Elphin, who is kidnapped and imprisoned by Maelgon, a neighbouring king. Taliesin goes to visit King Arthur at Caer Lleon, but on his way there arrives at the castle of Dinas Vawr, the stronghold of King Melvas. There he discovers, in the person of the king's butler, the famous Seithenyn, who was thought to be dead years before but who had contrived to escape on the night of the great catastrophe. Here Peacock makes use of the third legend, for Taliesin learns from Seithenyn that Arthur's wife, Queen Gwenyvar, who has been missing for some time, is actually a prisoner in the castle of King Melvas. The remaining chapters describe the efforts of Taliesin, seconded by Seithenyn, to persuade Melvas to restore Queen Gwenyvar to her husband. When this is finally accomplished, King Arthur compels Maelgon to release Elphin, and Taliesin marries Melanghel and becomes Chief of the Bards of Britain.

Here, for once, Peacock undoubtedly attempted some careful plotting, and the result only throws into relief his weakness. He has no sense of narration, of the steady march forward of events, of the way in which action can be ordered to produce the best effect. He really cares for nothing but the scene—and for the scene he has the eye of a comic dramatist—and so he jumps from one to another with little regard for the conduct of his plot. Even those readers who have read *The Misfortunes of Elphin* several times—and to read it once is inevitably to read it again—have probably only a very confused notion of the actual story and could not say what object Taliesin has in wandering from Dinas Vawr to Caer Lleon, from Caer Lleon to Dinas Vawr. Moreover, the action is continually held up by the songs, of which there are far too many. Peacock could not resist the temptation to translate every old Welsh ballad that came his way, and find a place for it in his tale. The best verses in the book are his own, of course, being the now famous *War Song of Dinas Vawr,* which is sung by the heroes in the hall of Melvas—

who were celebrating their own exploits in sundry chorusses, especially in that which follows, which is here put upon record as being the quintessence of all the war songs that ever were written, and the sum and substance of all the appetencies, tendencies, and consequences of military glory:

THE WAR SONG OF DINAS VAWR

> The mountain sheep are sweeter,
> But the valley sheep are fatter;
> We therefore deemed it meeter
> To carry off the latter.
> We made an expedition;
> We met a host, and quelled it;
> We forced a strong position,
> And killed the men who held it.

On Dyfed's richest valley,
Where herds of kine were brousing,
We made a mighty sally,
To furnish our carousing.
Fierce warriors rushed to meet us;
We met them, and o'erthrew them:
They struggled hard to beat us;
But we conquered them, and slew them.

As we drove our prize at leisure,
The king marched forth to catch us:
His rage surpassed all measure,
But his people could not match us.
He fled to his hall-pillars;
And ere our force we led off,
Some sacked his house and cellars,
While others cut his head off.

We there, in strife bewild'ring,
Spilt blood enough to swim in:
We orphaned many children,
And widowed many women.
The eagles and the ravens
We glutted with our foemen;
The heroes and the cravens,
The spearmen and the bowmen.

We brought away from battle,
And much their land bemoaned them,
Two thousand head of cattle,
And the head of him who owned them:
Ednyfed, king of Dyfed,
His head was borne before us;
His wine and beasts supplied our feasts,
And his overthrow, our chorus.

All the other verses in the book pale before this chorus,
whose mingled brevity and droll heartiness point the
satire. Most of the other songs we could very well
spare.

This "war song" gives the key to the whole story,
which displays the same mingling of drollery and irony.
The romantic elements in the author himself are now

carefully subdued so that the tale is animated by a single spirit throughout. As usual, Peacock makes use of the past to satirise the present. He takes a delight in reversing popular judgments. Thus we are accustomed to think of ordinary life in such a distant dark age as being very much inferior to the common life of our own day. Peacock takes care to upset this complacent judgment. But we are also accustomed to think of its outstanding personages, its Arthurs and the like, as being magnificent romantic figures. Peacock reverses this too, turning his kings into so many brigands and their bards into so many drunken sycophants. His most sustained passage of ironic comment in any work is to be found in the sixth chapter of this tale, the chapter called *The Education of Taliesin*, of which we may quote the first six paragraphs or so:

As Taliesin grew up, Gwythno instructed him in all the knowledge of the age, which was of course not much, in comparison with ours. The science of political economy was sleeping in the womb of time. The advantage of growing rich by getting into debt and paying interest was altogether unknown: the safe and economical currency, which is produced by a man writing his name on a bit of paper, for which other men give him their property, and which he is always ready to exchange for another bit of paper, of an equally safe and economical manufacture, being also equally ready to render his own person, at a moment's notice, as impalpable as the metal which he promises to pay, is a stretch of wisdom to which the people of those days had nothing to compare. They had no steam-engines, with fires as eternal as those of the nether world, wherein the squalid many, from infancy to age, might be turned into component portions of machinery for the benefit of the purple-faced few. They could neither poison the air with gas, nor the waters with its dregs: in short, they made their money of metal, and breathed pure air, and drank pure water like unscientific barbarians.

Of moral science they had little; but morals, without science, they had about the same as we have. They had a number of fine precepts, partly from their religion, partly from their bards, which they remembered in their liquor, and forgot in their business.

Political science they had none. The blessings of virtual representation were not even dreamed of; so that, when any of their barbarous metallic currency got into their pockets or coffers, it had a chance to remain there, subjecting them to the inconvenience of unemployed capital. Still they went to work politically much as we do. The powerful took all they could get from their subjects and neighbours; and called something or other sacred and glorious, when they wanted the people to fight for them. They repressed disaffection by force, when it showed itself in an overt act; but they encouraged freedom of speech, when it was, like Hamlet's reading, "words, words, words".

There was no liberty of the press, because there was no press; but there was liberty of speech to the bards, whose persons were inviolable, and the general motto of their order was Y GWIN YN ERBYN Y BYD: the Truth against the World. If many of them, instead of acting up to this splendid profession, chose to advance their personal fortunes by appealing to the selfishness, the passions, and the prejudices, of kings, factions, and the rabble, our free press gentry may afford them a little charity out of the excess of their own virtue.

In physical science, they supplied the place of knowledge by converting conjectures into dogmas; an art which is not yet lost. They held that the earth was the centre of the universe; that an immense ocean surrounded the earth; that the sky was a vast frame resting on the ocean; that the circle of their contact was a mystery of infinite mist; with a great deal more of cosmogony and astronomy, equally correct and profound, which answered the same purpose as our more correct and profound astronomy answers now, that of elevating the mind, as the eidouranion lecturers have it, to sublime contemplations.

Medicine was cultivated by the Druids, and it was just as much a science with them as with us; but they had not the wit or the means to make it a flourishing trade; the principal means to that end being women with nothing to do, articles which especially belong to a high state of civilisation.

And so on to the end of the chapter, a sustained piece of ironic persiflage not easily matched in the whole range of English Literature.

This is the manner throughout the tale, except in certain passages that are either broadly humorous or descriptive and picturesque. Here is our introduction to the King of Caredigion:

Gwythno, like other kings, found the business of governing too light a matter to fill up the vacancy of either his time or his head, and took to the more solid pursuits of harping and singing; not forgetting feasting, in which he was glorious; nor hunting, wherein he was mighty. . . .

And again:

Gwythno and his subjects went on together very happily. They had little to do with him but to pay him revenue, and he had little to do with them but to receive it. Now and then they were called on to fight for the protection of his sacred person, and for the privilege of paying revenue to him rather than to any of the kings in his vicinity, a privilege of which they were particularly tenacious. . . .

At this point it may be as well to remind ourselves that Peacock is frequently described as a Tory satirist. The particular brand of Toryism that inspired these and similar gibes has not yet, however, been revealed to us. Of the office of Lord High Commissioner of Royal Embankment, we are told:

He executed it as a personage so dominated might be expected to do: he drank the profits, and left the embank-

ment to his deputies, who left it to their assistants, who left
it to itself.

When Taliesin arrives at Caer Lleon, the author blandly
observes:

The city, which had been so long the centre of the
Roman supremacy, which was now the seat of the most
illustrious sovereign that had yet held the sceptre of Britain,
could not be approached by the youthful bard, whose genius
was destined to eclipse that of all his countrymen, without
feelings and reflections of deep interest. The sentimental
tourist (who, perching himself on an old wall, works himself
up into a soliloquy of philosophical pathos, on the vicissi-
tudes of empire and the mutability of all sublunary things,
interrupted only by an occasional peep at his watch, to
ensure his not overstaying the minute at which his fowl,
comfortably roasting at the nearest inn, has been promised
to be ready), has, no doubt, many fine thoughts well worth
recording in a dapper volume; but Taliesin had an interest
in the objects before him too deep to have a thought to
spare, even for his dinner.

And later:

The mild precepts of the new religion had banished the
ferocious sports to which the Romans had dedicated the
amphitheatre, and, as Taliesin passed, it was pouring forth
an improved and humanized multitude, who had been enjoying the pure British pleasure of baiting a bear.

Again, after the bards have been singing:

Besides the single songs, there were songs in dialogue,
approaching very nearly to the character of dramatic poetry;
and pennillion, or unconnected stanzas, sung in series by
different singers, the stanzas being complete in themselves,
simple as Greek epigrams, and presenting in succession
moral precepts, pictures of natural scenery, images of war
or of festival, the lamentations of absence or captivity,
and the complaints or triumphs of love. This pennillion-
singing long survived among the Welsh peasantry almost

every other vestige of bardic customs, and may still be heard among them on the few occasions on which rack-renting, tax-collecting, common-enclosing, methodist-preaching, and similar developments of the light of the age, have left them either the means or the inclination of making merry.

The great figure of the book is Prince Seithenyn, who is Peacock's finest creation, with the possible exception of Dr. Folliott. The latter is the more rounded and carefully modelled character, but the Prince is a creature of larger growth, one of those huge comic characters whose lives, of which we only obtain a glimpse, are vast epics of folly. Seithenyn is one of the immortal topers of literature. We never meet him out of his cups; he is always reeling ripe. Undismayed by any change of fortune so long as there is liquor to be had, he staggers through the tale flourishing his golden goblet and for ever crying *Gwin o eur*—"Wine from gold." He is just as happy and uproarious as a butler as he was as a High Commissioner of Royal Embankment. He is always on hand to proffer the cup: "Take a little more," he cries. "That is the true quantity. Wine is my medicine; and my quantity is a little more." Does his friend, the Abbot, see a difficulty ahead? Then Seithenyn has his remedy: "Screw yourself up with another goblet, you will find the difficulty smooth itself off wonderfully. Wine from gold has a sort of double light, that illuminates a dark path miraculously." The Abbot finds a certain argument "nearly true". "A little more," Seithenyn tells him, "and it will become quite true." Usually we find him at that stage of intoxication which might be called the argumentative and dialectical, when the drinker, floundering in a happy alcoholic mist, attempts an almost insane clarity of speech and a strictly syllogistic method of reasoning. Like all Peacock's characters, his talk has a crisp rhythm, a tang, and this adds just the necessary sparkle of salt to his speech and gives it the perfect flavour of absurdity. Every considerable speech he makes carries with it a most imposing air of reason, and yet every one ends by being nonsense, matter so tangled that it is impossible to unravel it. Among the great bibulous fools of literature, he takes first place as a dialectician, and in their Land of Cockaigne he must have been immediately appointed official apologist. As a specimen of his characteristic topsy-turvy method of reasoning, there is nothing better than his denial of his own death in the eleventh chapter, when Taliesin discovers him, the supposedly drowned Prince, acting as butler to King Melvas:

The stranger goggled about his eyes in an attempt to fix them steadily on Taliesin, screwed up the corners of his mouth, stuck out his nether lip, pursed up his chin, thrust forward his right foot, and elevated his golden goblet in his right hand; then, in a tone which he intended to be strongly becoming of his impressive aspect and imposing attitude, he muttered, "Look at me."

Taliesin looked at him accordingly, with as much gravity as he could preserve.

After a silence, which he designed to be very dignified and solemn, the stranger spoke again: "I am the man."

"What man?" said Taliesin.

"The man," replied his entertainer, "of whom you have spoken so disparagingly; Seithenyn ap Seithyn Saidi."

"Seithenyn," said Taliesin, "has slept twenty years under the waves of the western sea, as King Gwythno's Lamentations have made known to all Britain."

"They have not made it known to me," said Seithenyn,

"for the best of all reasons, that one can only know the truth; for, if that which we think we know is not truth, it is something which we do not know. A man cannot know his own death; for, while he knows anything, he is alive; at least, I never heard of a dead man who knew anything, or pretended to know anything: if he had so pretended, I should have told him to his face he was no dead man."

His greatest appearance, however, is made earlier, when we meet him as High Commissioner of Royal Embankment. The scene in which Prince Elphin and Teithrin (the officer who has complained about the embankment) visit Seithenyn in his castle to remonstrate with him, is one of the best scenes in all Peacock's fiction. Outside, the grey tides are crumbling away the ruinous mound of the embankment, but inside the castle, the torches blaze, the sound of harp and song bursts through the doors, and wine and wassail go round. High above his jovial followers, who are celebrating in chorus the circling of the mead horns, sits the great Seithenyn, flourishing his golden goblet and already deep in his cups. "You are welcome all four," he cries to his two visitors. When he learns who they are, he tries to stand up but can only wave Elphin into the seat beside him:

Elphin seated himself at the right hand of Seithenyn. Teithrin remained at the end of the hall: on which Seithenyn exclaimed, "Come on, man, come on. What, if you be not the son of a king, you are the guest of Seithenyn ap Seithyn Saidi. The most honourable place to the most honourable guest, and the next most honourable place to the next most honourable guest; the least honourable guest above the most honourable inmate; and, where there are but two guests, be the most honourable who he may, the least honourable of the two is next in honour to the most honourable of the two, because they are no more but two;

and, where there are only two, there can be nothing between. Therefore sit, and drink. GWIN O EUR: wine from gold."

Elphin motioned Teithrin to approach, and sit next to him.

Prince Seithenyn, whose liquor was "his eating and drinking solely", seemed to measure the gastronomy of his guests by his own; but his groom of the pantry thought the strangers might be disposed to eat, and placed before them a choice of provision, on which Teithrin ap Tathral did vigorous execution.

"I pray your excuses," said Seithenyn, "my stomach is weak, and I am subject to dizziness in the head, and my memory is not so good as it was, and my faculties of attention are somewhat impaired, and I would dilate more upon the topic, whereby you should hold me excused, but I am troubled with a feverishness and parching of the mouth, that very much injures my speech, and impedes my saying all I would say, and will say before I have done, in token of my loyalty and fealty to your highness and your highness' house. I must just moisten my lips, and I will then proceed with my observations. Cupbearer, fill."

"Prince Seithenyn," said Elphin, "I have visited you on a subject of deep moment. Reports have been brought to me, that the embankment, which has been so long entrusted to your care, is in a state of dangerous decay."

"Decay," said Seithenyn, "is one thing, and danger is another. Everything that is old must decay. That the embankment is old, I am free to confess; that it is somewhat rotten in parts, I will not altogether deny; that it is any the worse for that, I do most sturdily gainsay. It does its business well: it works well; it keeps out the water from the land, and it lets in the wine upon the High Commission of Embankment. Cupbearer, fill. Our ancestors were wiser than we: they built it in their wisdom; and, if we should be so rash as to try to mend it, we should only mar it."

"The stonework," said Teithrin, "is sapped and mined: the piles are rotten, broken, and dislocated: the floodgates and sluices are leaky and creaky."

"That is the beauty of it," said Seithenyn. "Some parts of it are rotten, and some parts of it are sound."

"It is well," said Elphin, "that some parts are sound: it were better that all were so."

"So I have heard some people say before," said Seithenyn; "perverse people, blind to venerable antiquity: that very unamiable sort of people, who are in the habit of indulging their reason. But I say, the parts that are rotten give elasticity to those that are sound: they give them elasticity, elasticity, elasticity. If it were all sound, it would break by its own obstinate stiffness: the soundness is checked by the rottenness, and the stiffness is balanced by the elasticity. There is nothing so dangerous as innovation. See the waves in the equinoctial storms, dashing and clashing, roaring and pouring, spattering and battering, rattling and battling against it. I would not be so presumptuous as to say, I could build any thing that would stand against them half an hour; and here this immortal old work, which God forbid the finger of modern mason should bring into jeopardy, this immortal work has stood for centuries, and will stand for centuries more, if we let it alone. It is well: it works well: let well alone. Cupbearer, fill. It was half rotten when I was born, and that is a conclusive reason why it should be three parts rotten when I die."

The whole body of the High Commission roared approbation.

"And after all," said Seithenyn, "the worst that could happen would be the overflow of a springtide, for that was the worst that happened before the embankment was thought of; and, if the high water should come in, as it did before, the low water would go out again, as it did before. We should be no deeper in it than our ancestors were, and we could mend as easily as they could make."

"The level of the sea," said Teithrin, "is altered."

"The level of the sea!" exclaimed Seithenyn. "Who ever heard of such a thing as altering the level of the sea? Alter the level of that bowl of wine before you, in which, as I sit here, I see a very ugly reflection of your very good-looking face. Alter the level of that: drink up the reflection: let me see the face without the reflection, and leave the sea to level itself."

"Not to level the embankment," said Teithrin.

"Good, very good," said Seithenyn. "I love a smart saying, though it hits at me. But, whether yours is a smart saying or no, I do not very clearly see; and, whether it hits at me or no, I do not very sensibly feel. But all is one. Cupbearer, fill."

"I think," pursued Seithenyn, looking as intently as he could at Teithrin ap Tathral, "I have seen something very like you before. There was a fellow here the other day very like you: he stayed here some time: he would not talk: he did nothing but drink: he used to drink till he could not stand, and then he went walking about the embankment. I suppose he thought it wanted mending; but he did not say anything. If he had, I should have told him to embank his own throat, to keep the liquor out of that. That would have posed him: he could not have answered that: he would not have had a word to say for himself after that."

"He must have been a miraculous person," said Teithrin, "to walk when he could not stand."

"All is one for that," said Seithenyn. "Cupbearer, fill."

"Prince Seithenyn," said Elphin, "if I were not aware that wine speaks in the silence of reason, I should be astonished at your strange vindication of your neglect of duty, which I take shame to myself for not having sooner known and remedied. The wise bard has well observed, 'Nothing is done without the eye of the king'."

"I am very sorry," said Seithenyn, "that you see things in a wrong light: but we will not quarrel for three reasons: first, because you are the son of the king, and may do and say what you please, without any one having a right to be displeased: second, because I never quarrel with a guest, even if he grows riotous in his cups: third, because there is nothing to quarrel about; and perhaps that is the best reason of the three; or rather the first is the best, because you are the son of the king; and the third is the second, that is, the second best, because there is nothing to quarrel about; and the second is nothing to the purpose, because, though guests will grow riotous in their cups, in spite of my good orderly example, God forbid I should say, that is the case with you. And I completely agree in the truth of your remark, that reason speaks in the silence of wine."

And here the gentleman, rashly attempting a gesture, falls down and has to be carried to bed.

There is more than one level of humour in this scene. The first level is that of topical political satire. The scene may be accepted as a Radical satire of the contemporary Tory attitude towards Parliamentary reform, and it is a fact that Seithenyn's defence of his policy of doing nothing is a parody of certain speeches of Canning's against reform, in which that states-man praised the existing British Constitution just as Seithenyn praised the crumbling embankment. The sec-ond level is still one of satire, but now we have left the immediate political reference and can discover in the scene the opposition of two familiar types of mind. Seithenyn becomes a caricature of those conservative-minded persons who will not have anything changed, partly because they have a real veneration for the past but more especially because they are both timid and indolent. Conservatism in general is the butt. There is a third level underlying these, and this gives us absolute humour in place of satire, not touching off a given situation nor ridiculing a certain mode of thought, but working—or rather, exploding—through character. Seithenyn dominates the scene and captures us just as Falstaff does in the scenes allotted to him. We see Seithenyn trying to make his reason serve his idleness, his intellect minister to his thirst, piling duty and common sense on the altar of boisterous good fellow-ship, dexterously keeping his happy seat in Cockaigne. He is a smaller, drier Falstaff, with a dialectic of his

own in place of the fat knight's nimble and astonishing
wit. We are sorry when he disappears in the storm and
are equally delighted when he pops up again, in the
manner of all comic characters, quite unexpectedly later
in the tale. Here, then, Peacock is no more a satirist
than Shakespeare is in the comic scenes of *Henry IV.*,
for Seithenyn can be enjoyed even though we forget
the existence of Canning and Parliamentary reform, of
Tories and Radicals : he is primarily the creation of
humour.

In this little tale Peacock's style is seen at its best.
There is no need to give further quotations to illustrate
its ironic piquancy and delicate pungency. A crisp
rhythm, a perfectly grave manner, a slight heightening
of language, a curious little "smack" in each sentence,
suggesting a faint and curiously droll over-emphasis in
enunciation if we think of the prose being spoken, these
are some of the devices by means of which he obtains
this effect. But his style, like any personal style, escapes
final analysis ; it is a tone of voice ; and the very restraint
of the voice, its even tones, only serve to heighten the
effect of the bland sarcasm and the lurking drollery that
find their way into almost every sentence. It is, too, a
curiously timeless style, not to be dated by either its
vocabulary or structure. Its balance and restraint may
suggest the eighteenth century—and some of his more
elaborate descriptive passages in the novels have a very
definite eighteenth-century ring about them—yet on
examination it proves to be quite unlike any style of that
century, not excepting that of Swift or Fielding, the
two most likely models. And in this tale it is not only
the grave ironic banter that is finely turned. The picturesque scene following that in which Seithenyn defends

himself, the scene of the storm and the escape from
the crumbling castle during the night, is unusually well
done. There is no attempt at the grand romantic manner, which would have been out of place even if Peacock could have achieved it, but in spite of the author's
reserve, his rather stately progress, it is not only
well-knit and finely turned, but really makes a vivid
picture throughout. Here is the conclusion of the
chapter:

> The bard, who had somewhat of a picturesque eye,
> could not help sparing a little leisure from the care of his
> body, to observe the effects before him: the volumed black-
> ness of the storm; the white bursting of the breakers in the
> faint and scarcely-perceptible moonlight; the rushing and
> rising of the waters within the mound; the long floating
> hair and waving drapery of the young women; the red
> light of the beacon fire falling on them from behind; the
> surf rolling up the side of the embankment, and breaking
> almost at their feet; the spray flying above their heads;
> and the resolution with which they impinged the stony
> ground with their spears, and bore themselves up against
> the wind.
> Thus they began their march. They had not proceeded
> far, when the tide began to recede, the wind to abate some-
> what of its violence, and the moon to look on them at
> intervals through the rifted clouds, disclosing the desolation
> of the inundated plain, silvering the tumultuous surf,
> gleaming on the distant mountains, and revealing a
> lengthened prospect of their solitary path, that lay in its
> irregular line like a ribbon on the deep.

It is all very deliberate, of course, every noun finding
its adjective rather too regularly and easily, and there
is nothing of that "constant slight surprise" in which
some people have found the secret of a fine style. But
it is clean, deft craftsmanship in prose, and it would be
impossible to match it in all the fiction of the later

'twenties, when the tale was written. As for that other and more characteristic manner of his, that style of grave banter, wise mischief, salted with irony and sparkling with fun, it is neither to be matched nor imitated: it is all his own, one of the clear voices of English prose.

CHAPTER VIII

HIS HUMOUR, HIS REPUTATION AND INFLUENCE

PEACOCK is a treacherous subject for criticism. He is one of those authors who, in their wilfulness, eccentricity, originality, leave a very definite impression on the mind, but nevertheless are very difficult to "place". He cannot be pinned down by a brief definition. The simplifications of criticism have continually allowed his spirit to escape. Thus he is frequently referred to as a Tory satirist, but the shortest examination of his works and character will show how inadequate, how downright misleading, this label is. It is true that he always displayed certain Tory characteristics, notably a violent mistrust of mob rule: "I am more afraid of deference to popular clamour than I am of anything under heaven," he once declared to a Parliamentary committee. And, like most scholars and humorists, he was strongly conservative in non-political matters, disliking change and believing that the old ways are the best. A political satirist, however, must be seen against the background of his own time. Now, even when he had published *Crotchet Castle,* the last but one of his novels, Peacock was regarded as a Radical in his own day, and not without good reason. The chief targets of his political satire had been Tory politicians and policies. One novel of his, *Melincourt,* is in parts, as we have seen, nothing but a Radical pamphlet. And nowhere does he share the usual Tory belief in a strong Government and old institutions. Yet we cannot go to the other extreme and make a real Radical out of him. Indeed, we might say of Peacock as a politician what he said of James Mill as a man: "He will hate what you hate and hate everything you like." Peacock hated everything the Radicals hated and hated everything they liked. As much might be said of his attitude towards the Tories. He was both Radical and Tory negatively, and that is why he has been claimed by both parties. That, too, is why he has puzzled the people who have looked a little more deeply into the question, such as his contemporary, Lord Houghton, who tells us that "the intimate friends of Mr. Peacock may have understood his political sentiments, but it is extremely difficult to discover them from his works". We have no evidence that those friends were any more enlightened. The political sentiments of Peacock were those of an aristocratic individualistic republican Radical with a strong Tory bias, whose good pleasure it was to be always against the Government. It will be agreed that this attitude hardly belongs to practical politics.

Thus Peacock is not a political satirist in the ordinary sense at all. He has not the usual desire to discredit one system or party and so indirectly exalt another. He is not a political thinker using wit as a weapon. Political life in general, particularly the incongruity of theory and practice, affords him material for satire, and so he becomes a satirist of politics, which is not quite the same thing as being a political satirist. He makes it his business to laugh at the incongruities and pretences and absurdities of this world, and the field of political life provides him with a fine crop, and a tempting target in the person of the canting politician. It is absurd that people should boast of their Parliamentary institutions and yet defend the existence of rotten boroughs. It is equally absurd that people should talk solemnly of Government when they are merely at the mercy of popular clamour, the silly catchwords of a mob. But his satire goes further than this, especially in such passages of ripe irony as we have already noted in *The Misfortunes of Elphin*. Government, political power itself, is incongruous and droll. It is incongruous because, notwithstanding our pretensions, it is nothing but superior might. It is droll because it is might always more and more artfully disguising itself as right. How absurd it is that rational beings cannot contrive anything better! How ridiculous they are when they pretend, in spite of the facts, that they are contriving something better! That is really Peacock's attitude. Like many another humorist, he may be said to be at heart an anarchist. Alternatively, we can see him again, as we did in a previous chapter when we examined his character, as an idealist, either disillusioned or too timid to speak out directly. The basis of his political satire is a secret comparison of this real world with some ideal one, such as the Republic of his beloved Plato. His view of actual political life hardly differs from Shelley's. Both of them see the real and ideal worlds in sharp contrast, but the ardent poet is inspired by the belief that a few strokes would transform the real into the ideal, whereas the satirist has lost that belief (if he ever had it) and so takes refuge in mockery. It is idle to try and mend the world, he says in effect, and so let us laugh at it.

This is the secret of Peacock's attitude. Any explanation of him that fails to remark the baffled idealist will be inadequate. Thus, Lord Houghton's view of him as an eighteenth-century man cast up into the nineteenth century will not do; it misses what is essential in Peacock. He has nothing of that rather solemn rationality and that love of over-simplified first principles which are characteristic of that earlier century, and he has a romantic gusto and a kind of intellectual high spirits which are equally uncharacteristic of that century. We do not fare any better if, following other critics, we regard him merely as a man of letters who happened to be also a man of the world or, if you will, the spokesman of plain common sense. That he was a man of the world and had abundant common sense is evident from his life, but it is much less evident from his literature, so whimsical and crotchety itself, so brimmed with queer high spirits, that men of the world have passed it by and plain common sense has merely stared in bewilderment. It was precisely when he sat down to write, and assembled in his Nightmare Abbeys and Crotchet Castles the fantastic creatures and odd notions in which he delighted, that Peacock ceased to be simply a man of the world, that he gave common sense a holiday. Otherwise he would never have bothered his head about such people and such notions. Such a person as some of his critics have sketched for us would never have produced—for his own good pleasure, too, it must be remembered— fiction of so unusual and whimsical a character. It is Peacock's peculiar relation to ideas, loving them and yet not being able to accept them, it is his attitude towards the enthusiastic theorist and the crank, to whom he is always attracted but whom he can never join, it is the baffled idealist in him, taking refuge in laughter, that explain why his fiction takes such a form and why his satire and humour have this distinctive character.

When we talk of him "taking refuge in laughter", however, we are referring to his mind's secret motives, its inmost springs. We do not mean to imply that there was any sense of strain, that his laughter was forced, that he deliberately, knowingly, turned satirist to protect himself, as so many rather proud, timid and self-conscious persons frequently do. After all, Peacock enjoyed laughing. He had wit and delighted in exercising it. He wished to make use of his sense of humour just as he wished to make use of any other sense. Wit, satire, irony, were his diversions. These are obvious facts and yet they are very frequently overlooked. Peacock himself overlooked them when he came to discuss the subject of comic fiction. Like more than one comic writer before him, he makes the mistake of ignoring the play element in comic writing and of over-emphasising the serious reformatory purpose of its authors, so that we are left to suppose that every time a comic writer sketches a droll scene he sees himself castigating folly and remedying social abuses. This is, of course, to take far too utilitarian a view of Comedy, and to mistake the character of its authors, whose real motives cannot be found on this level of social reform. The comic writer casts about and finds a number of targets so that he can exercise his wit and create laughter, and it is only afterwards that he discovers that these targets of folly were really a public danger and that he himself was inspired at the time by a serious reformatory purpose, that he does not enjoy and welcome folly but only wishes to banish it from the world. In reality, he laughs at the world, just as the romantic poet cries out in wonder or despair at it, for his own good pleasure, instinctively expressing himself in this way. What we should ask about him is not what purpose he had in mind but why his pleasure should take this form, how he comes to find in wit and laughter his characteristic means of expression. In examining Peacock's character, we have tried to answer these questions. He himself must have known in his heart of hearts that his view of comic writing was a partial one and did not really cover his own practice. There is more of himself in that speech of the Friar's in *Maid Marian*:

The world is a stage, and life is a farce, and he that laughs most has most profit of the performance. The worst thing is good enough to be laughed at, though it be good for nothing else; and the best thing, though it be good for something else, is good for nothing better.

There speaks the humorist. Ironically enough, many of Peacock's critics have fallen into the same error in their treatment of him, and have exalted the satirist with a serious purpose at the expense of the genuine humorist in him, though it is the humorist that has kept his work alive.

There is a valuable reference to Peacock in Shelley's *Letter to Maria Gisborne*. It concludes:

> . . . His fine wit
> Makes such a wound, the knife is lost in it;
> A strain too learned for a shallow age,
> Too wise for selfish bigots; let his page

> Which charms the chosen spirits of his time,
> Fold itself up for a serener clime
> Of years to come, and find its recompense
> In that just expectation.

The first phrase is very significant. This widening of the wound until the knife itself is lost in it marks the transition from the satirist to the humorist. The peculiar character of Peacock's wit does not allow him to remain a satirist, making a neat incision with the knife of purposeful and reformatory satire, but turns him into a humorist, who no longer seeks to mend the world but simply laughs at its incongruities. It is here that he parts company with Shelley, who wanted his friend to use his wit for the purpose of reforming the world and delighted in the most polemical chapters in *Melincourt*. But Shelley, in one of those intuitive flashes of critical genius that mark this poem of his, recognises this progression of Peacock's. Whenever the satirist in Peacock is closely examined, as we saw when we considered his political satire, he is discovered merging into the humorist. The satire is so frequently double-edged or even triple-edged that it loses all polemical force and is seen to be absolute humour of a somewhat dry and sardonic character: the knife is lost in the wound.

We saw in the last chapter how a characteristic scene of his, that in which Seithenyn defends his policy of doing nothing, in *The Misfortunes of Elphin*, could be interpreted on several different levels, beginning with topical political satire and ending with absolute humour. A further example of the way in which his satire is indistinguishably merged into humour is provided by the figure of Sir Oran Haut-ton in *Melincourt*. Sir Oran, though he never speaks a word (and we think none the less of him for that, his companions being far too wordy), might be called the hero of the tale. He is always on hand at the critical moment, to rescue damsels in distress. He is triumphantly elected to Parliament. He is represented as being the soul of good-fellowship, gentle, chivalrous, accomplished. Society is clearly fortunate in possessing this Angola orang-outang turned baronet. We are at liberty to regard this figure as a satire upon the writers whom Peacock quotes in his footnotes, Monboddo and others, who held that the orang-outang was of our own species and testified to its virtues. Peacock takes them at their word by having an orang-outang transformed into Sir Oran Haut-ton and by dowering him with all the virtues and accomplishments variously ascribed to the animal. But now the satire becomes double-edged. Sir Oran is at once seen to be superior, in all the qualities that matter most, to the members of the new society in which he finds himself: he can not only claim to be of our species, but he can also claim to be an unusually fine specimen of that species. His virtues of the wild woods are sufficient to distinguish him in the company he keeps. If this is to be an ape, then on what do men pride themselves? Thus, before he has done laughing at Monboddo and the rest, he is also laughing at the pretensions of society in general, at a civilisation that cannot readily achieve the virtues ascribed to wild creatures of the forest.

But perhaps nothing will give us such a clear idea of his peculiar humour as the typical scene of his novels, the scene we always remember when we think of their author. We see a number of odd personages, each with his own theory, bundle of opinions, or strongly marked point of view, arguing and dining and passing the bottle. They argue, strenuously and at length, but they never reach any conclusions nor do they ever convince one another. Each one looks at everything from his own peculiar angle. These people may be said to hold no real communication with one another, and though they sit side by side and share the same decanters, they would seem to exist in different worlds. Never was there such an example of the way in which men can be separated from one another by opinion. Here, then, is a world that is governed by opinion, where intellect plays the leading part. Here is a world in which ideas alone are important. But when we examine the scene again, we are compelled to reverse this decision. These people have something in common, namely a delight in talking and eating and drinking. When, in Crotchet Castle, a sum of money was offered to them for the purpose of regenerating society, every man put forward his own scheme and dismissed all others until it was suggested that the money should be spent on deliberative dinners, a suggestion that found the whole company in complete agreement. The following scene is characteristic of them:

Mr. Cypress (*filling a bumper*)
This is the only social habit that the disappointed spirit never unlearns.

The Reverend Mr. Larynx (*filling*)
It is the only piece of academical learning that the finished educatee retains.

Mr. Flosky (*filling*)
It is the only objective fact which the sceptic can realise.

SCYTHROP (*filling*)

It is the only styptic for a bleeding heart.

THE HONOURABLE MR. LISTLESS (*filling*)

It is the only trouble that is very well worth taking.

MR. ASTERIAS (*filling*)

It is the only key of conversational truth.

MR. TOOBAD (*filling*)

It is the only antidote to the great wrath of the devil.

MR. HILARY (*filling*)

It is the only symbol of perfect life. The inscription "HIC NON BIBITUR" will suit nothing but a tombstone.

The show of reason is different with every individual, but the fact remains the same for all the company. Intellectually they are worlds away from one another, divided by fundamental differences of opinion, but nevertheless they all sit snugly together, completely at ease, not one whit disturbed in their rollicking good-fellowship. They are all alike in that they share the solidly good things of life, of which the wine may be regarded as the symbol. Their total disagreement in all intellectual matters does not really trouble them at all. A moment ago, this seemed a world governed by opinion, but now it seems to be a world in which opinion is of no importance. By exaggerating both sides of human life, Peacock has emphasised its contradictory nature, set in high relief its droll incongruity. This is the secret of his humour. It is there in the very first dinner he gives us, in *Headlong Hall*, in this characteristic touch that he repeats again and again:

Mr. Escot

Of course, sir, I do not presume to dissent from the very exalted authority of that most enlightened astronomer and profound cosmogonist, who had, moreover, the advantage of being inspired; but when I indulge myself with a ramble in the fields of speculation, and attempt to deduce what is probable and rational from the sources of analysis, experience, and comparison, I confess I am too often apt to lose sight of the doctrines of that great fountain of theological and geological philosophy.

Squire Headlong

Push about the bottle.

This fiction might be described as the comic prose commentary on the *Rubáiyát*. But we have not yet reached in it old Omar's final mood. We are still young and eagerly frequent Doctor and Saint and hear great Argument, and are still oscillating, like Scythrop with his two loves, between old barren Reason and the Daughter of the Vine. Peacock sets us hanging, as he himself was hung, in the mid-air between the upper realm of ideas and the earth of brute fact, and compels us to see the humour of being in this droll situation. It naturally follows that his greatest appeal is to those readers who can find their way into this mid-air, not being resolutely attached to either the realm above or the earth below, to those readers, in short, who share with him a certain baffled idealism.

It is not surprising that he has never had a large audience. His humour, though more searching and profound than is generally imagined, only operates within a very limited sphere, and in order that it should find expression at all it was necessary for him to create an artificial little world of his own. From this world of his the greater part of human life, with all its tangle

of familiar relations, is banished. His limitations as an
artist are so obvious that they are not worth stressing.
His imagination was so infertile that even within his
own extremely limited range, we find him repeating
himself more than once. It was also timid, for in
spite of his intellectual impudence, his mischievous
spirit, his touches of romantic feeling, he never allows
himself to make a really bold imaginative stroke. There
was something stiff, stilted, self-conscious, about him to
the very last. His sympathies were so narrow that his
humour always remains high and dry, as it were,
and never draws near to the heart of this life, never
comes close to tears. Such tenderness as he had only
finds expression in one or two lyrics, and is rigidly
excluded from his prose. And though irony is his
medium, it is always the deliberate irony of the commentator, and, unlike some greater artists, he never
rises to the height on which a whole world shot through
with irony is presented to the reader. There is no
need to tabulate any further limitations. We are only
saying that he was Thomas Love Peacock and not
Shakespeare or Cervantes. His humour may be a
lesser thing than theirs, but, nevertheless, it is good
and it is unique. There is no more original figure in
the whole of our literature. His work is indelibly
stamped with his personality down to the last comma.
He is one of those few authors whose names have been
coined into adjectives, for we do not hesitate to call a
certain kind of comic scene or a certain ironic style
"Peacockian".

A glance at his bibliography reveals the slow but
steady growth of his reputation. In 1837 four of his
novels were published in Bentley's *Standard Novels*

and Romances, and were reprinted twelve years later. In 1856 these four novels, together with *Melincourt,* which had been omitted before, were brought out again. In 1875 came the complete *Works,* edited by Henry Cole; in 1891 an edition of the novels was edited by Richard Garnett; and four years later they were edited by Mr. George Saintsbury for Macmillan's *Standard Illustrated Novels.* In the present century, the novels have appeared in various popular series of reprinted classics, and have even been offered to the public in one small volume, in a series of thin paper reprints. Their latest appearance has been in the fine Halliford Edition of the complete works, which may be regarded as being definitive. As his bibliography suggests, his reputation grew more rapidly towards the end of the last century, by which time the testimony of such critical admirers as Garnett and Mr. Saintsbury had not been without effect. During his own lifetime and for some years afterwards, however, he was extraordinarily neglected. There was an article on his novels by Spedding in the *Edinburgh Review* in 1839, but it does not mention their author by name. He has no place in Maclise's *Gallery of Illustrated Literary Characters,* and all the works of reference for the following thirty years either do not mention him at all or are very brief and very inaccurate. His death did not bring out the usual lengthy obituary notices, and it was not until the publication of the *Works* in 1875 that there was any general discussion of his work in the reviews. It is not difficult to see why an author now securely established as a classic, if only a minor one, should have remained so long in comparative obscurity. In the first place, Peacock did not court public notice. Much of his work was published anonymously, with long intervals of silence between the various volumes. He was not a man with a host of literary friends and of acquaintances of the Press; he did very little periodical writing himself; he lived a very secluded life, and even his work as an official rarely brought him before the public. If it had not been for the growing interest in Shelley, it is likely that he would have remained in even greater obscurity than he did. In the second place, his work, which could hardly have a wide appeal at any time, would certainly not commend itself to the taste of the mid-Victorian public. His nonsense would not suit their nonsense. The age had a taste for humour, but it was not the humour of Peacock, the comedian of ideas, the master of ironic persiflage. By this time, too, the earlier novels had lost all force as pieces of topical satire, but had not yet ripened into pure comedy, so that they would doubtless seem merely queer, stiff, old-fashioned, so many stale and stilted old jokes. Perhaps the most astonishing event in Peacock's career is the publication of his last novel, *Gryll Grange,* as a serial story in a magazine. This must be accounted the last, and certainly not the least, of *Fraser's* bold experiments. Remembering, then, how Peacock always held aloof and how opposed his work was to the literary fashions of the time, we may well be rather surprised to find he was sufficiently known and appreciated to have his novels included in such a series as Bentley's. It was, however, the operatic *Maid Marian* that led the way, whereas the far more characteristic *Misfortunes of Elphin,* which with *Crotchet Castle* represents Peacock at his best, had to wait forty-five years before it was reprinted.

The direct influence of Peacock has been almost negligible. One or two writers, notably W. H. Mallock in his *New Republic,* have borrowed his device of the country house filled with guests who are either caricatures of actual individuals or personified points of view. On the other hand, we may hazard a guess that his indirect influence has been very considerable, though naturally it is difficult to trace. There can be no doubt, however, as we have already seen, that Meredith was greatly in Peacock's debt, not only for a character or two, or a brilliant passage here and there of a Peacockian flavour, but for that interest in philosophical comedy which shaped his course in fiction. That charming and rather neglected volume of short stories by Richard Garnett, *The Twilight of the Gods* (which antedates the work it resembles most, that of Anatole France), suggests the keen student of Peacock. The same might be said of one or two volumes published within these last few years by younger writers. Indeed, the influence of Peacock is probably stronger at this present time than it has ever been before, and it is not unlikely that his reputation will soon be established with a far larger body of readers than his critics of twenty or thirty years ago would ever have dreamed of allotting to him. There are sound reasons for this, quite apart from traces of his influence in recent fiction. The tide has now turned in his favour. His prevailing mood has a marked resemblance to the prevailing mood of to-day. That baffled idealism of his which can only find its expression in irony and gusts of laughter, his habit of juggling with ideas while maintaining a cool scepticism, his sardonic attitude towards all pretentious and canting persons in authority, whether they represent vested interests or lead mobs, his determined anti-romantic flourishes that do not quite hide a wistful tenderness for romance itself—how far removed are these from the habit of mind and literary attitude so much in evidence since the War? We can hardly regard our own day as that "serener clime of years to come" mentioned by Shelley, yet Peacock's page may well find its promised recompense in this day. And our own wits have still something to learn from that page. They may discover in Peacock an attitude of mind not unlike their own, but they will also discover a quality that is hardly ever absent from his work and hardly ever present in their own—geniality. Peacock is as sunny and genial, as free from harshness and bitterness, as the good old wine he celebrated. Although there is a certain baffled idealism behind his laughter, it has not made him morbid, sour, misanthropical. In some respects the most sophisticated of our authors, he yet carries with him to the last a suggestion of the boy. He loves the open air and sunlight, and then high jinks in the evening. If he is the most intellectual of our comic writers, he is also the most kindly of our satirists. He is not one of those satirical wits who rout among the fundamental decencies and sanities and savagely scrawl across the common pattern of this life, leaving behind them a dwindling wonder among lovers and warmth among friends. He salutes—in Raleigh's phrase— "all that is simple and matter of affection", and only kindles into mischief when he is confronted with ideas or the antics of public figures. His most impudent caricatures are creatures so far removed from actual private persons that they are only huge and harmless jokes. Even the worst of them has his share of the bottle and the final chorus. He brings out rapier and cudgel and does lightning execution for our delight, but nobody is one whit the worse, and before he has done, we are all seated at the table in eternal good-fellowship.

INDEX